FAMILY SECRETS

FAMILY SECRETS

DON SMARTO

Also by Don Smarto

Justice and Mercy
Tyndale Publishers, 1986

Pursued
Intervarsity Press, 1992

Setting the Captives Free
Baker Books, 1994

Keeping Ex-Offenders Free
Baker Books 1995
Revised, Frontline Press, 2001

Lost and Found
Frontline Press, 2003

To order additional copies of **Family Secrets** or any of the above titles:

Write: PO Box 764499, Dallas, TX 75376-4499
Fax: (972) 572-8335
Call: (972) 572-8336
Web: www.youthdirect.org

To my mother,

who kept secrets to protect me

and shared them to guide me.

Published by Frontline Press
PO Box 764499
Dallas, TX 75376-4499

Printed in the United States of America

ISBN 0-930201-07-8 (Trade Paper)

Library of Congress catalog card number: 2004108981
Printed in the United States of America

First Printing, July 2004

Table of Contents

Introduction 11

1. I was the youngest 21

2. I was a bartender....................35

3. I was poor....................53

4. I was connected 69

5. I was invisible 93

6. I was angry....................109

   Photos 122

7. I was apprehensive 193

8. I was next in line 213

9. I was depressed 233

10. I was suspicious....................243

11. I was cut off 265

12. I am blessed 289

Epilogue 299

Acknowledgments

- Grateful appreciation to Sue Ann Reynolds, transcriptionist, typist, and friend, for her dedication to this project.

- To Kenneth Sewell for his cover design and book layout.

- Photos by Celicia Bolar (page 192, backcover) and David DeJong (pages 128, 137, 182)

- To the thousands of incarcerated juveniles I have shared this story with. May this book lead them to a better life.

Out of respect, the names of some of the people in this book have been changed.

Intro

Everyone has a story to tell. My story is not more important than your story. Mine may be different, but yours is just as unique.

What is your story? It's the sum total of all your experiences. It's comprised of everyone who loved you, everyone who did not love you, those who encouraged you and those who criticized you. Your life story is a mixture of the people who believed in you and the people who said you would never amount to anything. Your story is a combination of those who stuck by you in difficult times and those who kicked you when you were down.

Everyone has a story.

In 1990, part of my story (the refusal of tainted money) was printed in Decision Magazine. Immediately four major Christian publishers approached me about a book. I was 44 years-old at the time and thought myself too young to write my life story. But several friends persuaded me that the story could be an encouragement to many people.

So I began writing. My overriding goal was not to make myself a heroic character but to strive for transparency. I wanted the reader to see a real person with blemishes who made mistakes as well as a person who made good choices. I also wanted them to see the struggle and the clash with family values I experienced as a follower of Jesus Christ.

InterVarsity Press published **Pursued** in 1990. I remain grateful for their devotion to the project. Little did I know then how important the book would become to so many. **Pursued** continues to sell strong wherever I speak, and not a month goes by that I do not receive a letter or an email expressing gratitude.

The transparency (allowing people to see the good and the bad) became meaningful to many. Numerous people have contacted me sharing their struggles with culture and family and how my book gave them the courage to make the right moral and spiritual choices.

Thirteen years later people frequently ask, "Whatever happened to your son? Did he survive his heart disease? Did your mother receive Christ? Did you restore relationships with your brothers?"

Sometimes the questions are worded in a rather naïve fashion. "It all worked out, didn't it?" they will ask with the assumption that everything is now fine because people were praying.

As you will discover in **Family Secrets**, life is not like a movie. A screenwriter can put a happy ending on every story, but many times we have to live with difficult situations and persevere in the face of events and obstacles we cannot control or change. Unless you lived it, you do not understand the dynamics of a family with over 100 years of crime history. Unless you were raised as I was, you do not understand Sicilian grudges, hotheaded relatives and daily flares of temper.

This may surprise some, but while I told my story in **Pursued,** I did not tell the whole story. I did not intentionally hide facts. It is just that in the years following that publication I came to grips with realities I did not fully understand. In her late seventies and early eighties I had long and introspective conversations with my mother that filled in a lot of missing pieces. She revealed secrets.

One theme of this book is seeing the truth. That means the truth without explanations, defenses and rationalizations. The truth is not always pretty. The truth about our family is sometimes dark and disturbing. I discovered the true identities of "uncles," the real fate of missing people, the connection to infamous mobsters, my grandfather's hidden activities, the family's knowledge of legendary crimes and their own crimes. Most families, like mine, rewrite history. They naturally eliminate what makes them look bad, exaggerate some factors and even create new scenarios that are fictitious. They do this to pass on a purer legacy to their children and grandchildren. But in the process they lie.

Most of us beyond middle age know that there is no such thing as a perfect family. We all have at least one strange, if not "crazy," relative. We also come to the realization that life does not always turn out the way we planned or expected.

Seeing and facing the truth can come at any age from 15 to 50. Some people never see it. Some never see themselves as they really are because of spiritual blindness and denial.

So, what part did I leave out of my autobiography **Pursued**? Primarily my anger. At least in church culture, people do not talk much about being angry. They may say they were mildly upset or disappointed but forget that even

Jesus Himself had righteous indignation that erupted in anger. If in doubt, review his comments about religious leaders (Matthew 23:27-35) or the episode with the moneychangers in the temple (John 2:14-16).

I am not extolling anger as a virtue, but sometimes it is healthy to get honest with ourselves and realize we are angry, even angry with God for not preventing or controlling a hurtful situation.

Whenever I speak in a juvenile institution, I find that anger is a predominant theme. In fact, when I ask youth seated in a large group if they have an anger problem, I usually see a 90 percent show of hands.

My anger erupted in late adolescence. It hurt me. It hindered me. And it hurt those around me. But I mostly kept the reality locked away as a guarded secret. Often the anger turned back on myself and became a dark depression, which I lived with for more years than I want to count.

Now, I want to tell the whole story. My purpose in writing this book is to help some people, especially teenagers, to accelerate the process of seeing the truth. For some of us it took a long time to see things clearly. But I believe finding truth late is better than never. And sadly, some will never remove the mask they wear for fear people will see their insecurities and weaknesses.

If we are to grow, truly grow spiritually as well as emotionally, we must have people in our lives that hold us accountable. You may call that person a mentor, but basically it is a friend, someone you can confide in and someone you can tell the truth to without fear of judgment. I know that I need such people in my life. I have learned over the years that self-deception is easy and rationalization is common if not habitual.

We truly begin to grow when we face our motives and find that none of them are pure. We become mature people when we face our ambitions with honesty. We play many roles that result in wearing masks, but the ultimate objective of growth is becoming a real person with genuine feelings. I have learned that when you go through life pretending to be someone you're not, you only end up confused and shallow. I have also learned that facing the truth can at first be more painful than consoling, but it is ultimately liberating.

I consider it a privilege to minister to young prisoners. My ultimate desire is to lead them to God through a relationship with His Son, Jesus Christ. My method is always the same. I want to be a good listener and I want to hear their story.

It is always a poignant experience to talk with someone through a narrow food slot in a solitary confinement door. Whatever my choice of words, I am basically asking, "What is your story?" I just listen and learn.

Most cannot even begin to imagine how many troubled youth in our country have never had the opportunity to share their story with another person. Often the reason is as simple as no one took the time or cared enough to ask.

I find this particularly true for young prisoners. The criminality that brought them to prison had many contributing factors. Time and again I hear about fractured families, lack of fathers, and emotional, physical and sexual abuse. Over time, these youth have learned to hide their story. They bury it deep inside because sometimes it is simply too painful to consciously think about. There are also those who do not like to share their story when it makes the people they are "supposed" to love sound terrible or even evil.

As we build up trust and confidence and earn the right to be heard in ministry, it becomes simple to hear someone's story. We begin by asking, "What's your name? What do you like to be called? Where did you come from? Why did you move? Tell me about your grandparents. Why don't you talk about your father? How did you end up in a place like this?"

These are not simple questions that one can respond to with a simple yes or no. You may ask, "Why did you hang around with the wrong people?" and sometimes discover that a youth has never really faced the answer for themselves. They never asked, "What need did the gang fill? Did I ever feel I had choices?"

It is amazing what you can learn when you listen. Often within twenty minutes I can see the tears well up in a prisoner's eyes. It is in many ways redemptive and cleansing to tell your whole story to another person who really listens and cares.

I always consider it a privilege to share my story. Those who enjoyed **Pursued** and my other books have complemented me on transparency, a compliment I really appreciate.

Some have told me I am a good storyteller. I know God has given me a gift to fashion and craft a story. Because I am a visual person, I want my reader to see what I am seeing. That is what a story is, the powerful images of who we are, who we could have been, and who we dream of becoming.

Jesus told stories. He gave his followers visualizations. They did not have to memorize a list of religious rituals, rules and laws or a table of statistics and facts. The story of the lost coin, the prodigal son, the Good Samaritan and the lost sheep were visual, powerful and easy to remember.

I realize my story may have dramatic turns and twists that are not common to most, but what is common is we all have the God-given power to change. We all have pivotal moments in our life when we make important and decisive choices. When I was offered a large sum of money, it was a crossroads leading to a life of crime or the life in ministry I have today.

At any point we can choose to remake ourselves. Too often I hear people giving themselves excuses for bad behavior. "Well, that's just the way my father was." Or "I can't help it, that's the family I came from," or, "My temper's in my genes." It's that kind of thinking that makes for family and generational curses. The sins of the father are inherited by the sons when people give themselves excuses for continuing bad behavior.

If God truly has a plan for our life, and I believe He does, then not every plan or thought we have is worth pursuing. As we get older we learn that some dreams are pure fantasy, fueled by ego and even insecurity. Some dream of power, others of fame, and still others of fortune.

While history is filled with examples to the contrary, there are those who still believe that power, fame and fortune will be the solution to all of life's problems, but it never is.

We have a deep need for wholeness. As the early church father Augustine said, "There is a God-shaped vacuum in all of us that can only be filled by God." After we have gotten everything that life says is worth pursuing, money, possessions, notoriety, sex and drugs, we are ultimately left empty. That is because only God can fill that part which is incomplete in our lives.

This is not a psychology book, but it does deal with mental health issues. I have known and witnessed many people who have escaped life's deepest questions through a blur of alcohol and a haze of drugs and through blaming and criticizing others for their shortcomings.

I feel most sorry for the person who never makes mistakes, is not teachable, who believes there is nothing to learn from others, and has no need for role models or heroes. I know that we learn more from brokenness than our accomplishments. Fortunate as I have been to receive awards and recognition, I have learned far more in the valleys than I have on the mountaintops, and that is because God molds us through pressure.

You will discover in this book, as I did so slowly and painfully, my family's secrets.

I did not have the power to change myself. The forces of family were so strong that I could not have altered my path without divine intervention. In fact, it was more predictable and more logical for me to be where most of my family ended up and remain today. Because of the forces of family, tradition and history, today I should be deeply involved in crime, probably as a mob boss, or a prisoner, or dead.

If this reads like a mystery, that's because my family lived a mysterious life. My mother and I visited cemeteries over the years. The inscriptions on headstones and mausoleums triggered her memories. She took me to places she stood seventy years earlier surrounded by Model T Fords, infamous, dangerous characters, and relatives with dual identities. I could tell by her "far away" look that her memories had transported her back in time, and when I listened and imagined, I traveled with her.

My hope in writing this book is that you will find the same power I did to make good choices. Ultimately my story is a story about change. I am not a hero although I have had heroic moments. I am not a celebrity although I have had episodes of notoriety. I am not a world leader although I have influenced and changed some people in small parts of the world.

I am more like you than unlike you. During my life I have tried to relabel the bad, exercise denial and bury emotional wounds, but as I have faced the truth, healing has come.

After hearing my testimony in a juvenile prison, a 16-year-old boy wrote this to me:

> "Thank you for coming to visit us. You
> maybe won't remember me, but I was the

one who wanted to meet a blood relative of a powerful Mafia family.

I'm a gang member and I know it will lead me to my death or jail again for a longer time.

I know I'm wrong for saying this but I really looked up to your Mafia relatives. But now I know how God's power is.

You could have been a powerful guy. But God is telling me that if he saved your life, he's powerful enough to get me out of the gang.

I want to learn about what happened for you to change your ways. I'm glad God changed your life, otherwise I wouldn't ever met you."

Carlos

I was moved by this letter. God can use our stories in ways we can hardly imagine. So for Carlos and the thousands like him, I will share what happened to change my ways.

I was the youngest

I was the youngest.

I was the youngest of three boys and a first generation American, Italian-Americans, as we were known. The Italian language was spoken almost exclusively in my home and in a thick, Sicilian dialect that even the Northern Italians could not understand.

My parents spoke to me in English but all phone calls and conversation between each other were in Italian. From an early age, I was taught to be proud of my Sicilian heritage. I grew up in an Italian ghetto in Chicago's Little Italy where everyone on the block was a first or second cousin, uncle, aunt, or a *paisano*, which means a close friend from the same region in Italy.

We had friends, of course, from other parts of Italy: Abruzzi, Calabria or Naples. You were called *Napolitano* if from Naples, *Palermitano* from Palermo, and so forth. Because the Mafia originated in Sicily, those Italians from Chicago (in particular) got a reputation for being hoodlums and using machine guns.

Some parents tell their children bedtime stories about guardian angels and tooth fairies. Others tell stories about the exploits of family that were war heroes, pioneers, industrialists, or inventors. But the stories my mother told me were different. One of the earliest stories I remember was the story of my mother's aunt Teresa. It was 1886, and she was a single young woman in her early twenties who mended torn garments in her modest one-room apartment. It was a warm day in Marsala, Sicily, where my family originated. It was over 90 degrees by mid-day, yet a dry heat. The open shutters brought in dust and flies, the clatter of a horse and cart on the rough street below and the screams of a mother calling her child. But the noise outside was drowned out, as it had been many times before, by a couple shouting in a downstairs apartment. Only this time the shouts were becoming louder and more intense. There were loud noises and long pauses punctuated by staccato profanity.

A longer silence was suddenly interrupted by people running up the wooden stairs. The fighting couple burst into Teresa's room, the argument erupting once more. Before Teresa could comprehend what was happening, the woman grabbed a kitchen knife and stabbed her husband in the back. His face froze; his eyes bulged with shock, as he choked in the middle of a word, falling to the hard wooden floor, never to regain consciousness. The woman ran from the room, returning moments later with the *carabinieri* (the police). She pointed to Teresa and screamed, "*Omicida! Omicida!* (Murderer! Murderer!)"

News spread quickly through Marsala. Teresa Fiorino had been charged with murder—the motive; jealousy. Carmella,

Teresa's sister, rushed home when the news reached the bakery where she worked. Not trusting the courts for justice, the family would make their own plans quickly. That night the Fiorino family bribed a policeman and brought Teresa to a conscripted boat which took her to the island of Tunis to live in exile. Teresa died ten years later in 1896, never to see her family again, and Carmella never stopped mourning the loss of her sister. Carmella was my grandmother. And my mother Rosa always told this story with sadness emphasizing the injustice. Only years later did Mom reveal that Teresa was the dead man's mistress and the wife was *oobatz* (crazy).

As I grew up, my mother was careful to instruct me about all the famous Italians. Not just Michelangelo and da Vinci, the great sculptors and painters, but also the important American Italians. In the sports field there were the prizefighters Rocky Marciano, Rocky Graziano, and Rocky Barbella and baseball's Joe DiMaggio and Yogi Berra. And in the years to follow there was football coach Vince Lombardi and players Dan Marino and Joe Montana.

I heard much about the great New York Mayor Fiorello LaGuardia, for whom the airport is named, and in the years to follow, there was Anthony Scalia, the Supreme Court Justice, Mario Cuomo, the Governor of New York and, of course, Rudolf Guiliani, the Mayor of New York on 9/11.

When I was older I met Guiliani and also spent time with two famous Italians, Frank Capra, the Hollywood director and Joseph Bonanno, the real Godfather from New York, two ends of the moral spectrum.

I knew of the wine makers, Mondavi and Gallo, in California and Sebarro of Italian Swiss Colony wine. There was the great movie star Rudolph Valentino. And of course, Francis Ford Coppola who produced The **Godfather** films and Martin Scorsese who produced **Goodfellas** and **Casino**.

Because my mother was an opera lover, I heard the names of all the great Italian tenors, including Caruso, and the great conductor Tuscanini. There was Enrico Fermi who discovered atomic energy under a football stadium in Chicago, and according to my mother, "the real inventor of the telephone," Anthony Meucci. (Apparently Alexander Graham Bell got the patent first.)

In my history class there was no mention of Italians in colonial history, only those of English ancestry. Only years later did I discover the name Filippo Mazzei, a friend of George Washington who helped Thomas Jefferson fashion the Declaration of Independence with key phrases and basic ideas. Francesco Vigo was the first Italian to become an American citizen and helped to fund the Revolutionary War. No movies were ever made about these colonial Italian-Americans.

But many films were made about the "bad" Italians. While a teenager, a popular TV show called **The Untouchables** portrayed the Italians (Frank Nitti, Angelo Genna and Al Capone) as hoodlums. Reportedly, mobster Sam Giancana was so outraged by the TV show he put a contract out on the producer, Desi Arnaz, although it was never carried out. There were several motion pictures about Al Capone and his mob.

Before you can understand why the Italians, in particular the Sicilians, came to America in great numbers, you need to know some history. In what is referred to as the first wave of immigration between 1815 and 1880, immigrants were largely the Germans and the Irish. The English, of course, were already here.

The second wave brought 17 million new immigrants between 1880 and 1914. This is when my ancestors came to America. Four million of the immigrants were Sicilians. Sicily is a large island that looks like a ball being kicked by the boot of Italy. It had been conquered by many other countries; including Greece, Spain and France. Also the Northern Italians looked down on the Sicilians who were largely poor. They felt powerless and oppressed. The ground was poor for growing, and most Sicilians had no plumbing, only kerosene lamps and poorly constructed homes where chickens and mules lived on the first floor. A wild chicory plant, which made a salad called **escarole**, was a substitute when grain and other crops failed.

In the 19th century, Northern Italians layered twenty-two land taxes on the Sicilians. This created even more poverty. Those who had already landed in America wrote back and described what they saw in the small general grocery store; canned goods of foods from different parts of the continent. The Northern Italians had an expression, *Chi ha prato a tutto*, translated "Whoever has land, has everything." The expression was a form of mockery and it was enough to make the Sicilians, who made up 30 percent of all those who immigrated from Italy, want to leave their homeland.

At first they did not come to America. Some became fishermen in far off places like Australia and New Zealand. Others were welcomed to South America where workers were needed, however, 9,000 Sicilians died of yellow fever in South America.

When the day came to leave, the women cried as the steamships pulled out of the ports of Palermo and Genoa. There was an Italian saying on board, *Chi sta bene non si muove*, which translated means, "He who is well off does not move." Another reason for leaving their homeland was *morte di fame*, "dying of hunger."

The trip itself was not an easy one. My grandfather, Guglielmo Cappitelli, and my father Matteo Smorto came to America the same year, 1913, but on different ships. Both families came from Marsala. My father's mother and my mother's mother were actually first cousins. My father Matteo was a boy when he clutched the hand of his older sister, Vincenza, who was 14. With him were his other sisters, Teresa, who was 11 and Francis, who was 9. They were on the ship Perugia, which embarked from Palermo to

New York City. Two months later, at age 24, my
grandfather Guglielmo departed from Palermo on the
steamship Italia. Both steamships were similar in size,
approximately 400 feet long and 50 feet wide.

Little did my relatives know about the ordeal of crossing
the Atlantic by steamship. Few could afford a first-class
ticket. There were only 20 first-class passengers on the
Italia and 30 on the Perugia. My father, my aunts, and my
grandfather were all in third-class where there were 1,400
passengers crammed into what is commonly called
steerage. It was called steerage because it was below the
deck near the engines and the steering mechanisms. There
were no windows, it was crowded, noisy and smelly.
Third-class had triple bunks with only sheets separating the
men from the women.

In those days there were no stabilizers as are on modern
ships today, so any storm would create a very difficult 20-
day journey. Everywhere was the smell of vomit and urine,
and third-class passengers could only take turns in small
groups on the upper deck to get fresh air. Eventually my
ancestors got to *Lamerica*, as they pronounced it. They were
inspired by the sight of the Statue of Liberty, *La Statue
Liberta* but surprised to find that when the ship entered
port, the west side pier of Manhattan, only the first-class
were allowed to leave the ship and go directly into the city.
Ferries brought the other passengers back to Ellis Island, a
complex of buildings with a main hall. After 1880, 15,000
immigrants came through Ellis Island each day. Anyone
that appeared to be sick or have a disease was quarantined.
There was a common eye disease called trachoma that, if
found, had to be treated first.

My ancestors had few possessions, no furniture, just
whatever could be put in a small trunk or carried on the
backs of the parents and children. Strange uniformed
people, English, Irish and German officers, processed the
immigrants. Many Italians got the nickname WOP meaning
"without papers." Many had their names rapidly changed to

abbreviations or even to the name of the city or region they came from.

But the most difficult part of the journey still faced them. The Sicilians were crammed into a small area on West 22nd Street called "Hell's Kitchen," and my father and his family resided on Mulberry Street in that poor area.

When Dickens wrote about the London of Oliver Twist, there was a population of 175,000 per square mile in the slums of London. The Italians resided in a Little Italy of 300,000 per square mile, mostly on the east side of New York. It was called "Little Italy" because they continued to speak their own language and continued their traditions and culture.

The Little Italy where my grandfather Guglielmo settled had over 200,000 Italians living near Taylor Street and Blue Island by the time his first child, Rosa, was born. The cobblestone streets were lined with peddlers selling fruit, vegetables, and fresh fish from box stands filled with ice. Mixed with the clatter of streetcars and horse drawn carts was the distinctive Sicilian dialect. Clothes were hung from lines between buildings, draped out of windows, and on wrought iron fire escapes. Everywhere were the sounds and sights of scurrying children. *La Famiglia* became all-important.

My mother was raised in Chicago's Little Italy. My grandfather had come to America with only a small bundle of possessions. Speaking no English he could not get a good job, yet within ten years became wealthy. He built a barbershop with an impressive striped pole that was motorized. Their home was elaborately furnished. He was the envy of all the neighbors. He was the first to have a radio, not a crystal set like most, but a wonderful sounding radio in a large wooden cabinet. He was the first to own his own car, a 1927 Chandler. His wife had the finest clothes all coordinated with matching hats, gloves, purse and shoes. This was so different from how they lived in Sicily.

Because my grandfather had prospered financially (hardly on a barber's salary), their home was always open to family and friends. My grandparents were generous. Streets were filled not only with carts and vendors but the scene of many religious processions and feasts to Saint Rocco, the Madonna, and San Jennaro. There was food and wine in abundance, unlike the poverty of the "old country." My mother would often tell me of the large gatherings especially on Sunday mornings with the smell of home baked pastries and her favorite, lemon cream pie.

The men immigrated first and sent money back home, sending for the children and then their wives last. My father came without his mother. His father was stern and emotionally distant. He lived here several years before sending for his wife.

In the first few years of the Italian immigration, Italians sent back home 100 million dollars, which actually helped the Italian economy. When Benito Mussolini took power, he wanted to crush the Mafia, especially in Sicily. He did this by exiling over 1,000 ruthless criminals to America. That did not help the situation in the Little Italy communities across America. Soon there were pockets of large Italian populations in Chicago, Philadelphia, Boston, and New Orleans.

The early criminals were the "Mustached Petes." These were older Italians who basically used extortion. Extortion was asking for money as a form of insurance against violence. If someone did not pay up, they would break fingers or arms and would think nothing of breaking the leg of a small child.

One of the extortion victims was Enrico Caruso, the opera star. They threatened to slash his throat, so he paid thousands of dollars, over 20 percent of his salary, just to keep the Black Hand from hurting him. Most Italians did not dare go to the police. These were largely the Irish in Chicago and the Irish, English and Germans in New York. So the Sicilians developed a system to protect their own.

The first leaders in Little Italy were called the *padrone*, meaning "boss." Established authorities used the *padrones* to manipulate their own people. They were swindlers who charged for their service. They were even used as strike breakers. My grandparents did not like or respect the *padrones*.

Sicilian criminals, a secret society, brought with them the *omerta*, which was the code of silence. It simply meant that you never talked about the family or its business with strangers or authorities.

My Sicilian relatives had many superstitions. If you inferred anything that sounded like bad fortune, someone would immediately knock on wood. I can recall my mother throwing salt over her shoulder any time the saltshaker fell over. Mom would insist, "Bad things come in threes." If she heard of someone's death, she expected two more. When someone's eye was out of alignment (as was John Scalise's), it was referred to as the "evil eye." It was really a glass eye. Most men wore the Italian horn, the *cornu*, to ward off evil. Anselmi and Scalise, ruthless killers from the old country, dipped their bullets in garlic believing that the intended victim would die of poisoning if not by the accuracy of the shot.

Italian men were not religious. They would go when obligated to a funeral or a wedding or if an infant's godfather at a baptism, but one rarely saw them in church otherwise. Confession was something most had not experienced for years if not decades. Yet, even if gunned down on the steps of Holy Name Cathedral, they would hope for enough time for a good act of contrition and a priest to reach them with the oil of the last rites so they could go to heaven.

The Italian women were religious. Their culture was entwined with Roman Catholicism, which made them put more faith in the Virgin Mary and the saints than in Jesus. There was a saint for every country and every region. My mother always had a large statue of the nun Mother Cabrini under a glass dome. Francis Cabrini did not become a saint in my mother's lifetime, but she prayed to her nonetheless. My grandfather had encountered her on numerous occasions in Chicago's Little Italy. Francis Cabrini was more a social worker than a pietistic nun. Grandpa recalled her salvaging bricks from demolished buildings to build a children's hospital. He would tell my mother, "She was no saint. She would sweat and get angry and pressure people for donations." I guess his picture of a saint was someone with folded hands who floated off the ground. As an Italian immigrant, she cared about the high infant mortality rate in Chicago's Little Italy, child workers and the extreme poverty. She probably came closer to the concept of sainthood than most saints, perhaps an early Mother Theresa. But I remember him telling me in broken English, "She had a bad temper." (*Essere arrabbiate.*) He didn't like her. *Severo* (stern) and *brutto* (ugly) is how he described her.

The only saints I knew were statues in the church or those named for Italian feasts, but my grandfather actually knew a real saint (according to the Roman Catholic Church) and found her to be a stubborn and determined person, not unlike him.

I remember my grandfather mainly as an old man with white hair and a blackish white moustache. He spoke very little English, even into his eighties. I never saw warmth. He was proud, stern, and angry at times. The stories of his poverty in the old country, his coming to America with nothing but the clothes on his back and jobless, somehow did not match the family photos. Within a few years he built buildings, bought new cars, radios and a piano. Grandfather wore a diamond stickpin, diamond rings on his fingers, and immaculate white spats on black Italian patent leather shoes. He also wore starched collars, vest and ties. He had obviously done well for himself. But with a Sicilian temperament, he had much emotion, would be passionate in telling a story and had quite a temper when tested. His sudden wealth had an explanation, of course, which I will explain later.

As a child, I fondly remember the family orchestra in the "old neighborhood" on Austin Avenue. There were so many musicians in the family that after the evening meal, many instruments would appear. My uncle Francesco and father Matteo would tune their violins; my mother Rosa would be seated at the piano, my aunt and oldest brother held accordions, others warmed a clarinet, a trumpet, or a saxophone and, of course, mandolins. And if you did not play a formal musical instrument, Uncle Filipó passed out pots and pans from the kitchen. You would become part of the percussion section with a butter knife on a cheese grater or a spatula on a large pot. Grandpa Guglielmo was the conductor since he looked like Tuscanini.

Mom was very talented. By the time I was in college she sang in nightclubs around Chicago under the stage name Rose Carmen, mostly the Italian ballads sung strictly in Italian. Older relatives would tap their feet or nod their head, even teary-eyed, as *bello molte canzoni* (the many beautiful songs) would carry them back to memories of the old country.

She had a natural gift. Mom began playing the piano after my grandfather bought her a fine instrument. She played by ear, would hear a song only once and commit it to memory. She had a beautiful voice with a superb range. At an early age she played for family friends and relatives. Mom kept alive the traditions of the Italian songs from the "old country" in a Sicilian dialect.

In her early teens, at a community center of nearby Reese Park where the Italians played Bocce ball and gathered, she performed on an ongoing basis. People would flock to hear her play and sing. When she went to a home without a piano she would bring her accordion, on which she was equally proficient. As a child I would carry the heavy box and bring it to parties in people's homes.

When my mother and father were courting, Dad would play the violin, nicknamed the "squeak box," and Mom would accompany him on the accordion, called the "squeeze box." Relatives would join them on the mandolin, clarinet, and tambourine while my mother would provide the vocals with a strong voice. She never needed a microphone.

Mom would sing O Solé Mio, Funiculi Funicula, and Santa Lucia. In addition to the songs of Southern Italy, she would also sing the popular "Americanized" Italian ballads, including Arriverderci Roma, That's Amore, Three Coins in the Fountain, and Volaré. These were songs that were made popular by Italian-Americans including Tony Bennett (Anthony Bennedetto), Perry Como, Connie Francis (Concetta Franconero), Vic Damone (Vito Farinola), Dean Martin (Dino Crocetti) and Julius LaRosa.

One of the principle reason Italians were to marry other Italians was to keep the language, the food, the culture and the music preserved. Years later, when we moved to the suburbs, my mother would lament the loss of the old neighborhood, not the neighborhood of Mulberry Street in New York where she felt like a prisoner, but the old neighborhood in Chicago where everyone on the block was a relative or a *paisano*.

When I was five, I remember a wedding in the old neighborhood one summer. The newlyweds had retired to an upstairs bedroom. These weddings would last for two or three days. I was falling asleep about midnight when I woke up to the sounds of pots and pans rattling. The family orchestra was assembling. They had decided to go outside under the window of the newlyweds and serenade. I soon was fully awake and was given two lids that I would use as cymbals. It was as if all the adults were children. Uncle Filipo kept shushing everyone, "*Zito!*" (Quiet!) When the orchestra of twenty Sicilians was under the window, my stomach churned with anticipation. Filipó began conducting. On his downbeat, it was very loud. After a few minutes, a light came on, the window was raised and the couple leaned out, not disturbed or angry but smiling, laughing and singing along.

Then as spontaneously as the serenading began, cousin Giacomo decided to have a parade down the middle of the street. The smaller children danced beside the band as they played an Italian march. I hit the steel lids to the beat as we moved forward. I remember the excitement. It was a warm summer night and many lights began coming on in different apartments.. Again, no one yelled "be quiet" or "shut up." They were all *paisano*. People began flooding out of their apartments and homes in robes and slippers and joined the procession, well after midnight. We had a parade of over sixty people marching toward Reese Park.

Those were different times. No one called the police for us disturbing the peace. I could understand why Mom missed those days. It was comforting to think that you could go to the apartment above or directly across the street if you ran out of sugar or flour. There was always someone to talk to, always someone to watch your child. A fresh pot of coffee was always brewing. Almost daily someone was coming up your walk with a platter, sharing homemade bread, pastry or leftover pasta. When Dad moved us to the suburbs it seemed everyone else moved too. They went in every direction but east, since that was Lake Michigan. We were only several towns away, but the "old neighborhood" was gone. Only my godparents held out for ten years but finally moved to the "burbs."

After we moved to the suburbs, mother constantly talked about the old neighborhood. It was a place Mom said where she could cross the street to visit cousins Vita or Nicolo or next door to Uncle Filipo or Aunt Teresa.

Years later I looked at the address of the building I was born in and realized that it was on the same street that Ralph Capone, Al's brother, lived. Both the house that my grandfather built and Ralph Capone's apartment building were identical and relatively close to each other. Tony Lombardo was also a neighbor. He was head of the Sicilian Union before he was killed. And not too far away on the same street, Austin Avenue, was Al Capone's "party house" where he would meet girls, drink, and entertain politicians when not with his family. My grandfather visited, but not with his wife.

Most of my relatives were not wealthy but in one sense they were rich. They shared. As a child I felt warmth and protection from the older relatives. They spoke very little English and would pinch me on the cheek and say, "Gooda boy,"(*buona bambino*) then slip me a coin or a dollar for ice cream. As a child I didn't know what they did for a living. Many were hard working, honest people. And some, of course, were not.

One day Mom told me that her uncle Vito, a musician, was returning to his apartment when someone ran up and shot him in the back of the head, a Sicilian style hit. She insisted it was a case of "mistaken identity."

There was a lot of violence in the early years of my ancestors. There was always an explanation that included "business" or "self defense." No one in my family ever used words like "thug," "mob," or "mafia." The only important phrase was *La Famiglia* (the family), which wasn't meant in the way we talk about a TV sitcom family. It inferred loyalty and *omerta* (keeping quiet).

Being the youngest with my oldest brother 15 years older, my brothers knew more than I did and often stopped talking when I entered a room as I was growing up. I never understood what the secrets were about. I was not supposed to, at that point, as the "baby" (*bambino*) of the family.

2

I was a bartender

I was a bartender.

I was a bartender and was only eight years old. It's not
what you're thinking. I was not a bartender at the corner
pub or tavern.

We had a large wooden bar in our home and in the homes
of most of our relatives and *paisanos*. Our bar was stocked
with many bottles. I once counted over one hundred with
every hard liquor imaginable from vodka and gin to
whiskey and tequila. There was no beer, as Sicilians
preferred wine, at least years ago. My father and brothers
drank mostly hard liquor.

My brother Anthony and my father thought it would be "cute" to teach me how to mix drinks. I followed the bar guide and usually made the drinks stronger than called for, and that always pleased my customers.

I was a skinny little boy with dark hair and large brown eyes. I would carefully carry the heavy tray through a cloud of cigar smoke into a back room where a group of men played five-card stud poker.

Strangely, I was one of the few outsiders allowed in the room during the card game. I was a quiet child, did not signal any faces to other players or interrupt. The women were never allowed in the room where the men were playing cards. I remember the cigarette and cigar smoke literally hanging in the air, and the sound of the dealer shuffling the cards. The men would take a break from the card game to have fruits, nuts or a dessert, but I never saw them eat at the table although they did drink during the game. Along with the drinks I would bring coasters so none of the cards got wet. I don't recall anyone having wine during the card games, it was usually whiskey or Seven & 7 (7-Up mixed with Seagram's Seven, a *blended whiskey*).

The women would drink martinis and cocktail drinks like a Pink Lady. Part of it was the culture, and part of it was the ethnicity. Wine was for dinner, the "heavy" drinks were for later at night during the card game, and the social drinks were usually for the women or when guests first arrived before the meal. The men could obviously handle their liquor as I never saw anyone drunk. They never wanted to impair their thinking when the financial stakes were high during the card game.

There was often a large pile (the pot), a mixture of silver and bills, often with large bills, 20s and 50s. When one of the men had a winning hand, he would slam his revealed cards on the table and the silver would jump into the air. It always startled me.

I did not know most of the people around the table. There was my dad Matteo, my godfather Giovanni and one real uncle, Giacomo, but all the strangers were called "uncles," too. Whenever I asked my mother what they did for a living, she would always say "business."

There were no card games on Sunday. Traditionally, Sunday was reserved for family.

On Sunday afternoons my grandfather would take his family for a long ride to Mt. Carmel Cemetery. There they would spend several hours seated on folding chairs while having a picnic lunch at the gravesite of Rosa's great grandmother Rosa Casano, her grandfather Vincenzo Titone, Uncle Vito (killed execution style), and many more. The family called it "visiting the dead." It was not a morbid activity but a time to remember loved ones and teach the younger children by oral tradition.

My mother took me for visits to the cemetery from the time I was small, as young as four. It was like walking through a family scrapbook, in fact, many headstones had photos imbedded in glass.

Growing up first generation Sicilian-American, I witnessed displays of emotion and Old World traditions. By age nine I was an old hand at wakes. The Italian wake (funeral parlor visitations) was a continuation of the mourning culture in Sicily. Widows were required to wear black for a full year and many stayed in black for the rest of their lives.

Emotion and theatrics were high. I remember one wake in particular. The deceased name was Mario, and he had died suddenly of a heart attack at age thirty. The young widow alternately cried, screamed and swooned. Every time she calmed down, more relatives would walk into the funeral parlor and the emotion would erupt again. Even though my father would want to leave, my mother would always say, "*Aspettate un momento* (wait a minute)." She had a good seat near the front near the casket, and this was better than television. Mom and her cousins would say, "*Che s'fortuna!*

(What a misfortune!)" and "*E' peccato!* (It's a pity!)" and "*E' porco vergogna!* (A dirty rotten shame!)" They were not statements of faith but statements about bad luck and fate. Death had the appearance of finality to my family.

As a small child I did not understand the theatrics. The widow Marie would go to the coffin, touch Mario's face and his hair, saying, "You are the love of my life, Mario. What will I do without you?" Then the widow would suddenly erupt with anger and hit the chest of the corpse screaming, "*Alzati! Alzati!* (Wake up! Wake up!)" "Why did you leave me? How could you do this to me? *Tu bastardo!* (You bastard!)" At that point other women would run up, grab her and pull her back to a couch.

As a boy, I did not get it. Was she sad or angry? Like the weddings, the Sicilian funerals went on for three days and the funerals in the homes for three nights, as well.

The closing of the casket was the time that most relatives waited for. That was when the *Impresario di pompe funerbri* (funeral director) would come and close the lid for the evening. I don't mean to be crass but it was like *show time*. The ritual of closing the lid for the night would make the widow and the sisters of the deceased cry out and occasionally faint. Today, the visitation tradition among Americans is the courtesy of visiting the family and signing the book. Years ago, the wakes of my childhood were emotional events. Before going to the church there was the major closing of the casket (usually the last look at the deceased) at the funeral home. In the case of Mario's funeral, there were more theatrics to come. There was a High Mass, which meant long. There were altar boys holding candles. The priest filled the sanctuary with the sweet smell of incense as he circled the casket with an incensor (Thurible), and then sprinkled the casket with holy water (Aspergill), as nuns hidden behind a partition sang in Latin.

When I was young the funeral concluded at the gravesite, not in a sterile chapel, as is custom today. In the case of

Mario, the top half of the casket was opened for one last look. I was too short to see in but I heard the widow as she kissed the cheek of the deceased saying, "Don't leave me." Then the aging mother all dressed in black, also kissed the face of her son saying, "*Figu mio* (my son)." With hundreds of relatives in a circle, the priest completed his prayers, flowers were put on the lid of the coffin and each pallbearer took off his gray gloves and likewise placed them on the lid. Then I watched as the funeral director disengaged a steel mechanism and began to hand crank the casket lowering it into the ground. I watched this many times. I always thought that "six feet under" was very deep, but with a concrete vault and the added height of the casket, it was not deep at all. I was surprised that the top of the casket was barely two feet from the surface of the ground.

The widow kept shouting, "I want to go with you! I want to go with you!" Suddenly she bolted from her caretakers and threw herself into the hole. I heard a thud as she landed on the metal lid. She really didn't fall that far, so when men reached in, she was able to easily stand and be lifted out. It was the only time I ever saw someone throw themself into a grave, but I remember it well.

At the lunch following the burial, which was usually a banquet (an important Italian tradition), my mother would always say to my father, "Let's go back and visit." She would like to see the fresh grave covered with dirt and also visit the graves of other relatives. Mom was comfortable in cemeteries, yet she was uncomfortable with the thought of her own death. She would say, "I don't want to be in the dark. I don't want dirt on my face. What if it is cold?"

We would laugh saying, "You won't know, Mom."

And she would respond, "You know what I mean."

But she did like the thought of the entire body being under the ground. She would try to imagine what her uncle or her mother would look like years later and if the dress or suit they were buried in was holding up. Anthony declared he was an atheist at 19, and to get a rise out of my mother, he told her he wanted to be cremated. My mother considered that a great sin.

"You're not supposed to hurry the process, you are supposed to be sleeping," she would say, "not burned."

Then my brother would quiz her, "What about people who die in a fire?"

"Well, they had no choice," she would reply.

Then my brother Anthony would add, "What about people who drown in the ocean and are eaten by fish?"

At that point, she would want to change the subject. "This is too gruesome, let's talk about something else, like food."

"I was talking about food, fish food," Anthony replied.

Another memorable funeral was that of my mother's uncle Guiseppe. There were rows and rows of red brick buildings at the place Mom's uncle had lived. A male attendant dressed in white would bring Uncle Joe in a wheel chair to an outside pavilion. He was missing a foot and my mother told me, "He lost it in the war." Whenever I watched war movies, I imagined him being hit by a hand grenade lofted by a German soldier. He always seemed sad, as did my mother who would cry in the car on the way home.

Another time when we visited him, the rest of his leg was missing from just below his knee, wrapped in a large bandage. Again my mother said, "It was poisoning from the bullet still in him." Eventually Uncle Joe was missing both legs and one arm, and I remember a bandage around his neck and one around his remaining wrist. The red brick buildings, I discovered, were a veteran's hospital and he was confined to the mental ward. When Uncle Joe died, it was another large Italian funeral.

I discovered years later that he had diabetes and was losing limbs because of his disease. It was important for all the amputated limbs to be buried in the same plot, so he could get to heaven intact (an Italian-Catholic belief). But it was only after my mother's death, talking to Uncle Joe's daughter that she said matter of factly, "My dad killed himself." I was shocked. "At first he tried to cut his wrists and then cut his own neck with a steak knife, but eventually he got hold of a gun and shot himself." Two subjects our family never talked about were **depression** and **suicide**.

Another bedtime story my mother told me was about the funeral of my great grandfather Vincenzo Titone. He was my mother's grandfather. In the old days, few Italians died in hospitals. They preferred to have the doctor make house visits and provide a duty nurse. Pneumonia was usually the killer as they got older. And when they died in their bed there was no place to go, not a morgue or funeral home. Mom would say, "I remember the undertaker (*becchino*) coming to the house. He would put up a sheet and begin to work on the body right in the bedroom. I could smell the chemicals. He would dump things in the bathtub (presumably blood). Several men came and brought the casket and set it up in the living room. The undertaker, with the help of an assistant, would put the body in the casket."

Relatives would crowd into the small living room with the strong smell of flowers. "The immediate family," she told me, "always gave a large bouquet on a stand that was fashioned in a clock with the hands pointed to the exact time of death. There were electric pink torchlights on each side, flickering candles, and a large crucifix on a stand. No one could ever leave the body alone," she continued, "all through the night my sister and I would have to sit on a couch in the dark room looking at his body by the flickering of the candles. Sometimes it seemed as if he moved. I was usually scared," Mom said. Funerals in homes (occurring into the 1950s) were for three days and three nights. The tradition of the hearse briefly stopping at the home of the deceased is an American nod to the Italian tradition of funerals in the home.

When my mother and father were children, the infant mortality rate of the "Little Italy" on New York City's Mulberry Street and Chicago's "Little Sicily" on Taylor Street was high, so funerals were a common occurrence. So were photos of the deceased. I found many photos in my family album of children propped up. As a child, I thought they were sleeping. Only later did I realize the babies and small children were dead. I also found many other photos of the deceased, such as my grandfather laying in his coffin in our living room. The "final photo" was not considered morbid, but a tradition, something that belonged in the family album. An open casket was always preferred, but when there was a mob hit disfiguring the face, it was *"e' una vergogna"* (a disgrace) to have a closed casket.

Like the funerals, Italian weddings were elaborate, on a grand scale. There were as many as ten groomsmen and bridesmaids along with the maid of honor and the best man. The men wore formal tails, the women wore elaborate gowns and wedding dresses were handmade with elaborate, long trains. Older Italian women would hand sew the lace and brocade on the dress. No one ever rented a wedding dress or sold it. It was to be kept in the family and passed on to a daughter or daughter-in-law.

There was one wedding photo that was conspicuously absent from our album; it was a wedding photo of my own parents. In fact, it was nonexistent because there was no Italian church wedding.

When my mother was older she handed me a set of letters that she and my father had written to each other when he lived in New York and she in Chicago. The letters were romatic and at times passionate. They were second cousins, so no one suspected a love affair developing.

Rosa started writing him when she was 15 years old and it was obvious that she was infatuated with Matteo. My

mother often said, "Your father looked like Clark Gable."
Dad had large brown eyes, slick black hair and was
impeccably dressed. Mom had blue eyes, curly hair and a
figure worthy of a model. They both loved to dance but
could only legitimately dance together at weddings. They
were falling in love, but an Italian man always needed
permission from a woman's father to date, court, or even sit
together. No one thought of matching Matteo with Rosa.
My mother Rosa knew very little of Matteo's day-to-day life
in New York. She saw him as gentle and respectable during
yearly visits, but did not see him as a boxer and a gambler
possessed by a Sicilian hot temper. These were secrets she
was yet to discover.

Matteo and Rosa's love for each other was a guarded secret.
She had turned 16, and when they walked together there
were no chaperones. Rosa began dreaming of a storybook
wedding, years in the future. One evening Matteo just
came out and asked Rosa to marry him. She refused.
"*E'impossible*! (This is impossible!)" she exclaimed. There
were too many details to arrange for, bridesmaid's dresses,
wedding gown, food, and a reception hall. Upset by her
resistance, Matteo said, "*Addio*," and left her home abruptly.

The next day my mother was giving a piano lesson in the
parlor when she heard shouting and dishes crashing in the
kitchen. Matteo came through the back door. He was
drunk. As my grandparents Guglielmo and Santa and
Uncle Francesco tried to subdue him, Rosa rushed into the
kitchen. She saw it was difficult to restrain him.

The sight of this unknown Matteo, a wild man, frightened
her! His usually groomed appearance was gone; his clothes
disheveled and hair unruly. He was weaving and
stumbling into furniture. Matteo was a professional fighter
so holding him was nearly impossible. More relatives, my
aunt Josephine and Mom's cousins Angelo and Giacomo,
ran to the kitchen to help, grabbing his arms, then his legs.
Suddenly in his stupor, Matteo blurted out, "Rosa and I are
engaged!" Rosa was shocked, as were her parents.

"Is this true?" Guglielmo said, turning to his daughter. Rosa lowered her eyes to the floor and sheepishly said, *"Si e vero* (Yes, it is true)." Her father responded, *"Tratto in ingauno!* (We were deceived!)" Then he said to both Matteo and Rosa, *"Sei ancora troppo giovane.* (You are still so young.)"

My grandmother gasped *"Che sfortuna!* (What a misfortune!)" putting her hands to her mouth. Why this terrible break with tradition? How could this romance have blossomed under their eyes?

After Matteo was pacified, he slept the night on a couch under Francesco's supervision. The next morning, tired, *mezza morta* (half dead) and embarrassed, he was promptly put on a train back to Brooklyn. Rosa and Matteo's parents talked by phone. When all the blaming was put aside, the parents decided to *metterci una zappa* (make the best of the situation). They would allow the courtship to continue by phone and by mail while plans would develop for a proper wedding in two or three years. My mother worked on every detail of the large church wedding with her mother. *La primavera* (in the spring) when Matteo returned to Chicago, he stayed with an old friend, Sammy. My mother never liked Sammy. There were rumors about his profession: a loan shark, enforcer, a guy connected to the mob. No one knew for sure.

Whenever Matteo and Rosa met, there were now older Italian ladies, often widows who performed as chaperones. When they went for a walk, the chaperones were only a few feet behind. When they were sitting in the parlor; the chaperones were sitting in the same room.

One particular evening, Matteo picked up Rosa telling her they were going to see a movie. He called on short notice. It was 6 p.m. when he drove up in Sammy's car. She was surprised to find Sammy beside him. There was no time to find regular chaperones so my grandfather sent Rosa's younger brother Francesco along. But when the men stopped off for some beers, her brother Francesco stayed behind. Matteo gave him money to take a streetcar home. Matteo, Rosa and Sammy continued on alone, but instead of going directly to the movie theater they headed to a neighborhood Rosa did not recognize.

Slowly Matteo circled the same block twice. He parked in a dark area and fumbled under the seat. By the lights of a passing car, Rosa saw him pull out a large black gun. He checked the revolver to see that each chamber had a bullet.

"What's that for?" she asked nervously. "I got to catch a guy that owes me some money," he responded. Matteo left the car quickly, walked down the street and disappeared into the doorway of an apartment building. Rosa was scared. She did not talk to Sammy who was sitting in the backseat of the car. As she glanced back over her shoulder, she noticed that he was holding a gun on his lap.

Soon Matteo returned, walking briskly to the car. More to Sammy than to Rosa, he said curtly, "*Peggio per lui!* (Serves him right!) Let's get out of here."

At last they were on their way to the movies, she thought. But now they pulled up to a house on Taylor Street. As they did, Matteo turned to 16-year-old Rosa and commanded, "Get on the floor." She was too nervous to question. Huddled down on the floor, her heart pounding and her breathing labored, she thought she would faint. "*Silenzio*" (Silence), he intoned. This time both Sammy and Matteo got out of the car. It was getting late, which made her worry about what her parents might think. Soon the car door opened, Matteo and Sammy got in the front seat with Rosa still crouched on the floor between them.

"It's OK now," Matteo told her, "You can get up." As he peeled away at top speed, Rosa said, "Matteo, I want to go home." My father assured her that everything was fine; he had gotten the money owed him.

Now there was a third stop, Sammy's home. Rosa was bewildered. Sammy retreated and in minutes returned holding a small duffel bag, which he threw into the backseat. Sammy's mother came out, leaned into the car, gave Rosa a broad smile and said to Matteo, "*In bocca al lupo, Matteo,*" which meant "Good luck, Matteo."

Now sitting in the middle, with Sammy on her right and Matteo driving, Rosa kept quiet but her mind was a whirl of questions. As they crossed a bridge near Calumet City, she knew they were moving away from the neighborhood. The air was humid, the sky dark and the scenery distinctly rural. They were now in Indiana and it was almost midnight. Matteo announced they were headed for Crown Point, Indiana, where they would find a Justice of the Peace and get married. Rosa was shocked.

She had never contemplated eloping. What would her parents think? What about her wedding plans? As much as she loved Matteo, her overriding emotion was fear. She was naïve and gullible. Both Sammy and Matteo had guns and she was terrified by the memory of the enraged Matteo she had seen the summer before.

When the Justice of the Peace questioned her age, Sammy immediately pulled extra money from his pocket and put it in his hand. The brief ceremony began. This was not the wedding she had envisioned in an ornate church, surrounded by bridesmaids and wearing a beautiful white dress. The only witness and best man was a family "soldier." He was armed but had no camera. And that is why there is no wedding photo of my parents.

It was now two o'clock in the morning and Guglielmo, my grandfather, was becoming more and more angry. He paced and then looked out the front window to the street below. My grandmother, Santa, was wearing her bathrobe, pacing in the kitchen. She had *agita* (an upset stomach). Then my grandfather caught a glimpse of the streetcar stopping at the Austin and Grand intersection. "*Vedo Franco*" (I see Frank), Guglielmo observed. Their son Frank emerged, clearly alone.

In a moment of fury, Guglielmo let out a yell. Santa came running into the living room. He knew what had happened: his daughter had eloped. He assumed Rosa was a willing part of the plot.

"Where's Rosa!?" Guglielmo yelled at Francesco, grabbing him by his coat lapels.

Francesco did not know. He had stayed at the bar (although underage) for hours, afraid to tell his parents he failed to remain with his older sister. Santa pleaded with Guglielmo to calm down, but he stormed out the front door and ripped the sign for piano lessons from the front of the building and threw it into the street. Then he disappeared into the cellar only to emerge with a hatchet in order to break the piano into small pieces. His wife and children did all they could to hold him back as he was *girna diment* (going crazy). Now other relatives, cousins and aunts and uncles, were awakened and came to calm him.

The ten-minute ceremony was over and Matteo and Sammy were driving Rosa to a cheap hotel back in Chicago. Tears moistened her cheeks, not tears of joy but of sadness.

My grandmother was dwelling on the shame of the elopement to the family, but also knowing she would forgive the couple when they returned.

However, it soon became clear that Guglielmo's sudden calmness was based on a determination to act, not forgive. He told Santa he was going for a ride. She was petrified. Before he and one of his brothers left in his large sedan, he loaded one of his shotguns and put a handful of 12 gauge shells in his coat pocket. He was an avid hunter, but now he was hunting for his new son-in-law, my father. My grandfather made several stops forming a posse. In his Sicilian rage, he would have killed my father if only he had found him. One of his first stops was Sammy's house. He suspected that Sammy was involved, but no one gave him any information and that made him all the more angry. From that day forward, they never talked or associated with

Sammy or his mother again. My grandfather would refer to her as *u' pazzu* (the crazy one).

Mom and Dad had checked in under a false name at the South Shore Hotel in Chicago. They spent their four-day honeymoon isolated in a hotel room. Sammy brought them meals and sat on a chair outside their door wearing his gun in a shoulder holster. He was far more than the best man; he was Matteo's bodyguard. And a bodyguard was needed since Sammy and Matteo knew what Sicilian anger was like, especially an enraged father's.

The first morning, Rosa woke up hoping she only had a nightmare, but she knew it was real when she saw Matteo's revolver on the dresser. He had gotten word that Rosa's father had formed a group brandishing handguns and shotguns. That is when Matteo decided to take my mother back to Brooklyn. Boarding a train, The Empire Express, she had no idea she would be exiled from her family for the next ten years.

Married life for my mother began in a grimy little apartment on Market Street near the waterfront, a group of tenements called slums. She had never known poverty, as her family lived very well in Chicago. Her father had provided everything she needed: ample food, good clothes, and the latest appliances. Now in Brooklyn, Matteo was out of work and my mother found herself on welfare. She had been accustomed to abundant food in the pantry, but now she used food stamps and waited in line with other poor people. Mom spent so much of her time crying and complaining about missing her family that Matteo's older sisters and mother disliked her.

All was not sad, of course. When first married, Mom and Dad were part of the ballroom dancing circuit along with his brother Lou and his wife Rae. Mom would save money for a night out to escape her dreary apartment. No matter how poor, he would wear his best suit and she her one floor length gown. Mom would tell me picturesque stories of Roseland on West Fifty Second Street in New York City where they would dance during the big band era to the music of Glenn Miller, Jimmy Dorsey, and Benny Goodman.

Earlier mother was a *flapper*. As a young girl she wore the typical tight dress and fashioned her hair with "spit curls" using an iron. She danced to the music of the *Roaring Twenties* and the early thirties: the Black Bottom, the Charleston, and the Lindy Hop. My parents would go ballroom dancing and dance the Tango, the Foxtrot, the Waltz and the Cha-Cha during the late 1940s and 1950s. She often lived for Saturday nights to escape from her exile in New York's tenements to dance to a live orchestra and listen to the top crooners of the era like Russ Columbo.

I enjoyed listening to my mother's stories about the ballrooms. She would have a twinkle in her eyes, and I could tell she was seeing those days in her memories. I would hear the slang from my mother's era called "Jive Talk." From the Roaring Twenties came terms of endearment like "Baby" and "Doll," which my father said to my mother when courting.

The Smorto's of Brooklyn did not want the Cappitelli's of Chicago to know where their daughter was. One day while my mother Rosa was writing a letter home, Carmella, Matteo's mother, entered the kitchen and said, "What are you doing?"

Before Rosa had a chance to say a word, Carmella lunged to the table and crumpled the letter "I don't want her writing to her family!" Carmella exclaimed to Matteo.

Not having heard from their daughter in months, the Cappitelli family notified the police. The Chicago police, in turn, contacted the New York City police who sent a policewoman looking for Rosa. My father had changed his last name to Smarto (from Smorto) perhaps to make it difficult for the police to locate him. But one day the policewoman came to their apartment and asked Mom directly if she was being held against her will. Matteo, his mother and sisters were in the room. Rosa looked around at the solemn faces and told the policewoman softly, "No."

In the spring of 1935, Mom was expecting her first child, my oldest brother Guiseppe (Joseph). Matteo was working one or two days a week as a longshoreman on the docks. It was hard work and sporadic. He would spend his days off with friends gambling in the back of a local bar or "playing the ponies" at the horse track.

Because they were poor, when it came time for Rosa to deliver her first child, she had to go to the county hospital as a charity patient. At the time of delivery Matteo was at the horse track gambling. He was not there for the delivery, in fact, he did not see my mother or his first child for three days. My mother felt abandoned.

Dad's gambling increased. Mom had a beautiful statue of the Madonna, which he pawned in order to bet at the racetrack. He went to the racetrack to see the famous horse Whirlaway. This was one of the few times mother went to the racetrack with him by subway, but all day as he gambled he did not take out time to buy her any food and she went home hungry. Things got worse. The more he lost, the more angry he got. In one heated argument, he smashed the prized statue of the Madonna that had been bought back from the pawnshop. He replaced it but that one, too, was smashed during a subsequent argument. His irritability grew.

Secretly, Rosa was saving for train fare to visit her family in Chicago. She finally had $27, the price of a ticket, but when she looked into the cookie jar preparing to attend her grandmother's funeral she discovered the money was missing. Matteo had taken it and lost it gambling. Then her grandfather died and again there was no money to attend the funeral.

The experience in the county hospital was terrible for her, so in 1940 when she delivered my brother Antonio (Anthony), she did not go to a hospital but delivered the baby in her bedroom. Since the midwife could not be located, my father was the only one present and literally saved the life of his second child because the umbilical cord was wrapped around his neck.

Rosa was living in a rundown tenement trying to raise two boys but she became weak and feverish after the delivery. Because her immune system was depleted, she developed a serious leg infection. Finally her mother Santa made a trip to New York to care for her sick daughter, but all too soon she was returning to Chicago, without Rosa.

Rosa's in-laws did not visit often. Rosa and Matteo's apartment was too small for entertaining. However one day when the family was coming, Rosa made every effort to have everything just right. While she was cooking, a cab brought Matteo home. He was drunk. Matteo's sisters and brothers arrived soon after and put him to bed after a long struggle. When Matteo's parents, Vincenzo and Carmella arrived, they were told their son was sick.

The tiny apartment was so hot that after dinner everyone brought chairs to the roof of the building. While the group was relaxing in the slight breeze, eating nuts and sipping wine, Rosa heard a loud and fiendish laugh. Matteo was standing in the doorway that led to the roof. His silhouette was unmistakable in the light cast by the bare ceiling bulb behind him. Not until he began walking closer did they see the gun in his right hand. Rosa shouted, "Matteo, put the gun down!" His family said nothing. Only his younger brother Lou comforted Rosa, "Don't worry, he's not going to hurt anyone." Matteo went to the edge of the roof and began to fire the gun into the air. **Bang! Bang! Bang!** The sound echoed down the street. Matteo was not angry, just happy. **Bang! Bang! Bang!** Rosa flinched with each shot and covered her ears. She had not known Matteo still had a gun and wondered where he kept it. She tried not to show it but in the years to come she continued to live in fear of his temper and his gun.

There was another funeral in 1943, Matteo's mother died. A typical Brooklyn funeral was held in the home. Carmella's body was put in a satin lined metal coffin and placed in the parlor. The indirect torchlights cast a pallid glow in the room. There were flowers everywhere including the traditional clock. A rosary was entwined in Carmella's fingers. A small crucifix was placed against the open lid of the coffin and a large crucifix was on a stand next to the red vigil light. While Mom's sisters-in-law carried on with crying, screaming, and swooning, my mother could only think in her mind that her mother-in-law's death created the possibility of an escape to Chicago.

And so she finally did return in 1944 after ten years in exile. My oldest brother Joseph was nine and my brother Anthony was three. Everything on Austin Avenue looked the same, at least physically, but much had changed.

Rosa's younger sister, Josephine, a devout churchgoer, had met a divorced Russian Jew, an intelligent man she met at the opera who was formerly married to an actress. My mother was shocked that her only sister, faithful to the Virgin Mary Sodality, had denied her Catholic faith.

Music was mom's solace.

When they moved back to Chicago in the mid 40s, my parents frequented the Aragon Ballroom. The music in Chicago was called "Boogie-Woogie." During a trip to Florida (when my father wasn't at the Hialeah Race Track in Miami) they would go to the CopaCabana nightclub where they would hear the DeMarco sisters, comedian Joe E. Lewis, and a young team, Dean Martin and Jerry Lewis. The music and the entertainment were sporadic diversions from my parent's tense relationship. The nightclubs helped bring calm, if only for a time. Austin Avenue had changed and the people were different, too.

Much had happened in my family before I was born two years later, but those events would cast a long shadow on my life.

I was poor

I was poor.

I was poor but didn't know it.

I know that sounds strange. How could a person be poor and not know it? The reason is related to yet another family secret. There were a lot of things I was told were "normal," and as a child I believed them.

I was the youngest of three boys so *hand-me-downs* were common. As a result, I never had clothes that were bought for me except for shoes. I was self-conscious, especially in high school, of the faded flannel shirts, the pants that were too short and the patches my mother had sewn on elbows and knees. I had a boyhood friend named Hank and he invited me to his birthday party one summer. During a game every child had to take off their shoes. I remember my embarrassment when both socks had holes with toes protruding. Worn clothes, in and of themselves, would not have been a big clue to our poverty, but food was another matter, especially the lack of money to buy snacks and lunch.

I remember feeling badly about not having any money on those special food days in elementary school. There was the Barbeque Day, the Kiwanis Peanut Day and of course the white Good Humor Ice Cream truck came to the playground every noon with pied-piper bells. I would carefully count out a few nickels and pennies and invariably be short the price of an ice cream bar as the man in the white suit shook his head from right to left. It seemed every child had an ice cream bar or a Popsicle but me. I cannot recall more than three or four days in eight years that I could afford one.

A second grade teacher, Mrs. Hermanski, felt sorry for me. Not having the twenty-five cents for a bag of peanuts, she would always share her bag with me.

Barbeque Day was the hardest. The odor of the fresh barbeque sandwiches with chips and a piece of chocolate cake filled the classroom. I had the same daily jelly and white bread sandwich my mother made, which I grew to detest. I was a quiet "good kid" so did not protest.

At home, Mom explained how Sicilians back in the *old country* had to make do with what they had. She would explain how many of the Italian dishes came from a lack of meat and poverty, but our food became, in her words, *delicacies*.

To my knowledge, I was the only child in my neighborhood that labored at eating chicken necks, chicken feet and snails. The part of eating snails I enjoyed most was getting to play with them before boiling them. It was not until later in life that I realized the so-called *delicacies* were cheap. In addition to snails I was often served tripe. It was a strange, white-ish honeycombed meat (although I thought it was fish), another *delicacy*. I later learned it was the lining from a cow's intestine.

Mom had a habit while riding in a car to yell, *"Basedago!"* when she spotted a wild plant growing along the road. She would pick the leaves. In truth it was a dandelion plant. From the leaves she would make a salad. We never bought a head of lettuce that I can remember. These dandelion leaves were very bitter but saturated in olive oil and seasoned with pepper and oregano, they weren't bad. My mother would say, "We were very lucky to have passed that field" (a field of weeds). As a child, of course, I believed we were lucky.

My father was hardly ever at home. My mother told me he was working, so I got used to taking buses everywhere. Mom never learned to drive nor did we have a second car so it was just a matter of taking a bus, perhaps two or three buses. We had many transfers and the rides were long to visit a relative.

Our house was small, but at the time I was not making comparisons. There were only two bedrooms, so my brother Anthony and I slept in the same bed. My oldest brother slept on a pullout couch. In the 1950s although there was central air conditioning, we had one small window unit in the living room. Mom insisted that it cooled the entire house. It did not.

I remember the sticky, clammy feeling of always sitting on chairs and sofas that were covered in heavy vinyl plastic my entire childhood. Mom said they were being protected "to not wear out," but she never removed the covers.

We were certainly not the only family that watched television on a small black and white set with rabbit ears (antennae) of course. We finally got our first color TV set in 1968 and watched the few color shows available: **Disney, Bonanza** and **Lawrence Welk.**

As a family, we never went on vacations although we would visit relatives in New York many summers. We never stopped to visit "sights." We would drive straight through from Chicago.

The first hotel I ever stayed in was during my freshman year in college at a student conference I attended in St. Louis. I was amazed by the size of the room and the furniture.

Not having money started to take its toll when I was a teenager. Presents were sparse at Christmas "because there are children in India who have no presents," Mom said. I heard a phrase similar when I did not like the chicken feet, "There are starving children in Africa who wish they had this meal." I know my mother meant well. She was making the best of a difficult situation.

Other boyhood friends would get shiny metal fire trucks for their birthday and elaborate erector sets for Christmas but not me. The only good toy I had was an American Flyer metal train set that I was only allowed to play with Christmas week, then it was put into storage for the rest of the year. My father seemed to enjoy playing with it most. I never understood why I only had seven days to play with it. My mother's explanation, of course, was, "So it will last." There always seemed to be an adage or a phrase connected with the family rules.

Disappointment came early, when I was six I remember being excited about a gift Mom said she was going to buy for me. She would save change in a flour jar. "I saw this Ferris wheel, and when I have enough money I am going to buy it for you," she said one day. Childhood anticipation is more emotional and exuberant than that of adults. I would dream about the Ferris wheel. I remember seeing one in the window of a large department store. It was magnificent, metal with hand painted, detailed tiny people that would swing in their seats. It had a big windup crank that made it turn. The one I had seen was at least 15 inches high and very ornate. That is the Ferris wheel I dreamt about. I did not know my mother had seen the Ferris wheel she talked about not in a large department store but in a "Five and Dime."

The day finally came. She had taken a bus and was going to bring the Ferris wheel home. I remember vividly the sinking feeling when she pulled out of a bag a small plastic Ferris wheel only six inches high that I easily identified as belonging inside a parakeet's cage.

I know Mom was hurt that I was not excited. I felt guilty for a long time that I did not show more appreciation. But it was the first "expensive" toy that I dreamt about that became just another disappointment.

We seldom went to restaurants (my parents did go to clubs, which is another story), and I went to the zoo only once a year with my father. I looked forward to that although I never questioned why other children went three or four times during the year. Also, there was a small amusement park in Maywood called Kiddie-Land. By Disney standards it was miniscule, more like a traveling carnival. My father would buy a string of tickets, twelve in all. Some rides, like the miniature railroad, required two tickets. If my mother or father rode with me, four tickets would be consumed. There were small ponies that walked in a circle. They took two tickets, but most rides took one. Sometimes I would take a long time trying to decide what I wanted to do next, because when we ran out of tickets, we had to leave and go home. I wanted to please my parents and be a good son and obedient child, so although I was disappointed when the tickets ran out, I never openly challenged why, at twenty-five cents apiece, my father could not simply buy another line of tickets for an additional three dollars.

My mother would say, "Next year you can go again and maybe your father will buy more tickets." But he never did. It was always the same three-dollar limit, twelve twenty-five cent tickets. I assumed this rationing is what happened in most families and not knowing the family secret behind the frugality, I accepted it.

In high school the lack of money became more pronounced. I was very skinny. While we had a good school cafeteria and other students were ordering hot dogs, hamburgers and a piece of pie, all I had each day was one quarter. There was only one thing I could purchase for a quarter and that was one scoop of mashed potatoes with brown gravy. That and a glass of water was what I had for lunch everyday for four years.

There was a kind lady, Mrs. Rinaldo, who worked in the cafeteria and wore a white uniform. I'll never forget her. She must have known it was all I could afford because the scoop she gave me was extra large. And beyond that, she always had this broad smile for me. I looked forward to meeting her every day, even for that one minute when she said, "How're you doing today?" And I would say, "Fine." And she would say, "I hope you have a good day."

All these years later, I can still see her face and visualize her smile. While other kids had two and three dollars to spend on their lunch, what she really gave me was better than food, an encouraging smile. Her daughter, Mary Lou, was a classmate. One day during my senior year I saw Mary Lou in a hallway crying and leaning on a girlfriend. I later learned that Mrs. Rinaldo had died that day of cancer. I really missed her.

I realized that even on those days when she had pain or was weak from treatment or contemplated the fear of leaving her children early, she always had the energy to muster a broad smile for me. I suppose that is why I remember her name and her face so vividly forty years later.

Since I was told it cost too much to get a bus pass, I walked to school each morning and back home in the evening. It was about four to five miles and I enjoyed walking except for the cold Chicago winters, the wind and deep snow. Sig Swanson, a dedicated high school teacher who became a father substitute, encouraged me to go to college, but my mother informed me we had no money for college. At fifteen I started working on a maintenance crew in high school. East Leyden in Franklin Park had a large building. The crew was made up of men who looked very old, but were probably in their late 30s and 40s. There was a cloud of cigarette smoke, profanity and strong foul body odor around them. Together we stripped, waxed, and buffed tile floors until we finished every room in the building and then would start over. I guess being the youngest on the crew I got some of the "dirt jobs." One was called "punching the flues." There were cylindrical holes in the boilers and I had to stand on a scaffold with a long rod to punch out the soot. By the end of my shift I would look like a London chimneysweep with black all over my face.

I also worked with a maintenance crew in college my first two years in addition to getting financial aid. My mother gave me money from her savings as a singer (out of the flour jar). My father was not able to contribute to any of my college education. After the first two years I entered a Roman Catholic seminary and the Church paid for the rest of my college, graduate and postgraduate education.

I tried to understand all the penny pinching. One obvious explanation was that my parents had come through the Great Depression. They had struggled and learned to live on less. There were the many sayings and adages of my mother such as, "Money does not grow on trees," and, "Be thankful for what you have." There is, of course, no shame in being poor. Some are fortunate to be born into families that have money and some are not. Great and successful people have come from poor families as well as wealthy ones.

In my teens, I went to see many movies alone, but most of the films that we saw as a family when I was younger were at the drive-in movie theater because it was cheaper.

That was always an interesting experience. There was so much to see at the drive-in. I would look into other cars (there was ample "necking" and "petting"), watch people walking by, and sometimes sit on the hood or the roof of the car if it was very hot. Only later in life did I rediscover films that I did not truly appreciate because the sound was coming through a tiny speaker in a metal housing hanging from the car window. I saw *The Ten Commandments* on a drive-in movie screen. The sun had not yet set when the projectionist started the film so I missed the first thirty minutes, not to mention headlights obliterating characters on screen. I also saw the great chariot race in *Ben-Hur* at the drive-in. Years later when they released these films on video and then DVD with stereo and surround sound, I felt I was seeing the movie for the first time. The drive-in was cheaper than the movie theater, which may have been one of my father's motivations. It wasn't until (as a teenager) I began venturing into downtown Chicago and watching films in the grand old theaters built in the 1920s, the Oriental, the Bismark, and the Chicago Theater where Sinatra had performed on stage in the 1940s. While many have been renovated today, in the 1960s these gigantic palaces with statues, frescoes and incredible ornamentation went into decline. Plaster was falling, seats were broken and upholstery ripped, and I remember watching rodents scampering across the floor of the Chicago Theater. It helped me to understand why my mother often talked about the late 1920s as the "golden years."

My growing up years were anything but "golden years," more like tarnished metal.

One day, a few years after my father's death, I was looking in a shoebox that contained his artifacts, including my father's billfold. I looked at his pay stubs and later found others from the period of my childhood. Suddenly a family secret was revealed; we were not poor! In fact, from his salary, we were upper middle class. Why did I think we were poor?

My father had gone from being a union organizer to a high-ranking manager in production at Dr. Scholl's Shoe Company. Even by today's standards his pay was very good. The real secret was not the money he made but where the money went.

My father was a gambling addict. I knew he gambled but I never knew it was a compulsive problem. My mother was an enabler. An enabler is a person who (in addictions like alcoholism) covers for the person. They make excuses and do everything to keep from confronting the behavior.

As I began to look back, it all became crystal clear. We would go to my godfather's house several evenings a week. As a child, I was fighting to stay awake as it got late, I would see him and my father sitting beside a black rotary phone. I must have watched this scene a hundred times. They waited for the phone to ring, usually midnight, and one or the other would pick up the receiver quickly, just listen and write on a pad.

When you are five, six or seven years old, the behavior means nothing. But I learned that they were waiting for a tip on a fixed race. My father would go to several racetracks a week, all day Saturday at Arlington Park Thoroughbred Race Track, Friday night at Maywood Park Harness Race Track, Wednesday night at Hawthorne Harness Race Track and Monday, Tuesday and Thursday night play poker with other Italian friends, and as well as bets on races in New York, Florida and California in local bookie joints.

In the 1950s you could fix a race by paying off a jockey on a good horse to hold the animal back or give a drug to a long shot horse to speed him up, a horse with odds greater and winnings larger. Of course, this was illegal. Sometimes my father would win thousands of dollars and sometimes "the fix" backfired and he would lose thousands of dollars. My mother never really knew how much money my father lost, but it was substantial, just based upon the lack of grocery money or rationed Kiddie-Land tickets.

I recall my mother looking through the kitchen blinds every Saturday as my father would drive up about 7:00 p.m. after a full day at the racetrack. It was a reoccurring ritual. She could tell in seconds if he won or lost by how he walked. If he walked upright with a hint of a smile, he had won. If he lost, he walked slowly with slumped shoulders and eyes on the pavement.

When he won, he would enter the front door and throw money into the air. I saw 10s and 20s fluttering, covering the living room floor. In fact, the Christmas present my father would give my mother in good years was currency rolled up inside of a toilet paper roll. As she would unroll it, more and more money would pour out. In a bad year with heavy gambling loses, the bills would mostly be singles but in a good year they could be 10s and 20s and even an occasional $100 bill.

As a child I was elated when he threw money into the air. He would hug my mother and on that evening we would go to the Golden Horns in Melrose Park or the Black Steer Restaurant in River Grove for a meal out. I would like to say that we had those restaurant meals often but it was usually only twice a year.

When Dad lost, it was a bad evening. Smoking compulsively, he did not talk when he entered the house, although my mother quickly started nagging about the money lost. Soon a fierce verbal battle would start. There would be screaming and cursing. Dinner itself would be a war of slammed plates and slammed cupboard doors. As a child, those were times of incredible tension for me. I never associated it with the loss of money, however. My stomach would tighten and sometimes I thought they were arguing about me and I would carry guilt. I would hide in the utility room and say to myself, "I wish I was never born."

My father would pick up the daily racing form on the corner of Grand and Harlem after midnight every Friday night. I would be in the car returning from a card game at my godfather's house. Dad would study the track conditions and the horse's history like a science.

I know there are people who enjoy racing as a sport. I never enjoyed it because it brought too much turmoil and pain into our house. My father did not really enjoy the race anyway because of all the stress of the money he bet and often lost.

As a gambling addict, it was not just horses, of course. As a family we would play cards (always five card stud poker) and today it seems unusual that I had to put up real money from my piggy bank even when I was five and six years old. My father did not enjoy the game unless the stakes were real. He could never play a board game like Monopoly with fake money.

As a child, my father taught me to play *cards*. There was only one game, poker. While my Mom would play pinochle with her girlfriends (called *goomahs*), my father played five-card stud poker. I learned all the terms watching him and my "uncles" play.

All the *bluffing* takes place on the first card, which is face-down followed by the next four, face-up. The card down is called *the hole*. As a child I would watch with fascination the *ante*, the *pot* in the center of the table where the money was placed. It would start with a *seed*, which could be everybody putting in a five or ten dollar bill until they reached the *cap*, which was the last raise you could make before you *showed your hand*.

I would watch my father carefully study his cards, held very tightly. Then he would say with a raised voice, "Hit me." That's when he was ready for another card after his bet. My father's game had no *wild cards* and the only variation I would see would be the fifth card down.

He would let me look at his cards as long as I stood behind him, said nothing and my face showed no emotion. Dad would remain very cool and collected if he had a *straight flush* or *five of a kind*, which could easily win. Sometimes I would see him play with a *weak hand* but keep another player *in* just to make the *pot* larger. This, of course, was his *bluff*.

When he lost, he lost big because they (my uncles) would sometimes play with no *limits*. The big games would start with a $500 minimum and a $50 *raise*. The big moment was the *showdown* when all would reveal their cards. I can still hear Dad laugh with glee when he won the *pot* putting both arms on the table and swooping the change and bills toward himself in one quick movement. Those were about the only times I heard him laugh or saw him smile.

Often, I would fight sleep when I was eight or nine years old since I was working, serving drinks. The games would go until one or two in the morning, especially when the next day was the weekend. Dad would want to keep playing if he was winning but would also keep playing if he was losing in the hope of winning his money back. I never saw him get angry with any of his card partners, but he certainly got angry with his family. He would yell at me (when I was a child) if I did not *fold*, which was getting out of the game. If I had a *weak hand* (cards that could not win) and stayed in the game he would say, "That's stupid!" I realize he was trying to teach me the art of the game but I did not want to play. At times he thought I was *bluffing* by *raising* him, but if I was *drawing dead*, which was trying to win with a hand that could not possibly win, he would likewise be upset. His anger always included expletives. It took a toll on my self-esteem as I thought of myself as "stupid" and felt "shamed." My mother and I were never allowed to play with his friends. That game was dead serious. It really wasn't a game, not the way a child would think of Monopoly. It was strictly for the money. And one or more "uncles" would go home winners or losers. Occasionally people would put in the pot a piece of paper with an IOU; I imagine they paid up rather quickly.

But the game was never fun, at least for Mom and me. And at the end of the family game, my father, being the best card player, would slide a big pile of silver coins toward himself from the middle of the table with a broad smile as the game ended.

He never gave me my money back, either. He would actually keep the money. It was money I had saved in my piggy bank, yet Dad would tell me, "You can win it back when you learn to play better."

I realize today that was part of his addiction. Gambling was never fun for him, nor was it a game. It was his way of "making it rich and retiring early." Of course, his dream of early retirement was moving near a racetrack and gambling every day so it would never have ended.

A few times Mom encouraged me to go to the racetrack with my father on Saturdays and some evenings if it was a school holiday. That was not enjoyable for me. My father would study the racing form. Then as the race started, he would yell and scream for his horse to come in first. If he lost, he would rip the tickets into tiny pieces and curse: *Merda! Puttana!* and worse. It always seemed to me that I was invisible. He was preoccupied with his gambling. If he lost, which happened more than he won, I would sit in the car on the ride home and he would not say a word to me.

Sometimes I would sit in parked cars for an hour or more, as my father went into a small tobacco shop. I could not really see him in the shop but he told me to stay in the car and that is what I did. Later I realized that the back of the tobacco shop was a bookie joint. He was gambling on races in other cities.

Although everyone knew, his gambling was a family secret so no one was allowed to talk about it, certainly not as a problem. No one had the guts to confront my father. He had a violent temper and formidable skills with the fists of a former boxer.

All addictions ultimately cause the family pain because addictions are dead end routes. They lead to compulsive behaviors, loss of control, and in the case of gambling, a loss of substantial money that resulted in frustration, anger, and in my father's case, extreme aggression.

I guess it never occurred to my father that I was not eating well at school. He assumed my mother was making sandwiches for me each day, which after years of plain bread and jelly, I would quickly pitch. From faded hand-me-down clothes to sparse food, I accepted it as just a part of life.

My older brother Joseph soon picked up the gambling bug. He would lose money on card games, even betting on bowling frames. My father lost so much money as a gambling addict that there was little insurance money when he died and no inheritance to speak of, certainly no savings.

I found stacks of boxes in the garage of a booklet he had published and was selling by mail order titled *How to Win at the Races*. It seemed ironic to me that he had a formula for betting, understanding odds and winning that never really worked for him.

As Mom got older she revealed more family secrets to me. One secret was that during the ten-year period of exile in New York when my father was basically hiding from my grandfather, he was gambling on boxing matches, which he called "the fights," horse races and card games. During the first years of their marriage, he frequently went to the pawnshop. My mother told me sadly that he had pawned her wedding ring in order to gamble. Eventually he was able to purchase it back, but he also discovered money she was saving in a secret place, took it and lost it as well. She ended up not seeing her own family for many years, and upon returning to her family, her mother (my grandmother) died. I now realize that a lot of my mother's sadness as I was growing up was because we had little resources and she made do with what little money she could save. She was not able to confront the gambling addiction the way families can today. Most of the screaming matches were about his losses, although I did not know that at the time.

Where did the addiction come from? I don't know. Did it start young, as my mother would suggest? Perhaps. My mother would tell me that my aunts (my father's older sisters) would give him money when he was a teenager to gamble with. If so, I am sure that was only the tip of the iceberg. He stole money from his father as well at a shoe store where he worked, to gamble with.

For all the time he spent gambling, he never seemed to enjoy it except on those rare occasions when he won. Would our life have been different if he had saved the money? Of course. The true measure was not in what we might have gained in possessions but in a more stable and tranquil home environment without the persistent arguments. I was resentful when I first learned of my father's heavy gambling losses in view of the hard days of manual labor to pay college tuition, but I forgave him and eventually felt sorry for him.

If you have ever lived with someone who has an addiction, you know that they usually are the last person to know it. They are often powerless to help themselves. And when there is someone in their life who enables them or makes excuses for their behavior, then it truly becomes a family secret.

I was connected

I was connected.

I was connected and related to historical crime figures, some the subject of television programs and motion pictures.

Some have ancestors that came to America on the Mayflower. Others are related to colonial leaders or Civil War generals. But not my family.

Yes, there were those with titles like *captain* and others called *soldiers*, but not from the U.S. military and certainly not from military campaigns in Europe, Asia or the South Pacific.

Many *family* members were lost in wars but not fighting against the nations of Germany or Japan.

The enemies were at times German and Irish, but mostly they fought each other. It was not a civil war and certainly not ideologized.

They fought and died for money. They killed for business territory. They assassinated out of rivalry and revenge.

It was called the **Gangland Wars**. And the battles were mostly in the streets of New York and Chicago in the *Roaring Twenties.*

When my family immigrated to America from the cities of Palermo and Marsala, Sicily, they resided in those cities. My mother and her parents lived in Chicago. My father and his parents lived in New York.

The apex of the mob wars was from 1920 to 1935. Like many Italians, my family witnessed the carnage and attended over five hundred *soldier* and *capo* funerals.

Jim (Giacomo) Colosimo emigrated from Sicily in 1895. He became a Chicago street gang member eventually working as a street sweeper who aligned with political forces to become a precinct captain and eventually a ward boss. 2126 South Wabash was his famous Colosimo Café. The food was excellent, as was the backroom gambling and the girls on the second floor. Big Jim did well for himself and wore diamond cufflinks, diamond rings and tiepins.

One day in 1920 he got a threatening letter from the Black Hand *(la mano nera)*. They threatened to kidnap him, hold him for ransom, torture and eventually kill him if his relatives did not pay up. He understood the extortionists and knew that whatever money he gave them would only be the first of many payments. *"Di mai di sapere guando col piremo"*, a note said (You will never know when we *will* strike.)

Colosimo did not go to the police nor did he go to the powerful politicians he worked for. He went instead to his nephew, Johnny Torrio, in New York. Twenty-nine year old Torrio, a member of the Five Points Gang, came to Chicago at Jim's request. In the meantime, three Sicilian thugs went to Colosimo's restaurant office and told him he had only one day left to live if he did not fork over $25,000. A rendezvous was set up the next day under a viaduct on Archer Avenue. The three blackmailers were waiting for Colosimo when Torrio and three of his men with sawed-off shotguns jumped out of autos at Torrio's command and finished them off.

Some time later another thug named Little Jimmy Cosmano called "Big Jim" saying, "I'm goan' keel you!" Torrio, who had stayed in Chicago to defend his uncle, said it was time to bring in two "good men" from New York. He brought in his cousin Frankie Yale and another trusted companion, Al Capone. Their bullets solved Big Jim's problems. But even with friends like Torrio and Capone, Colosimo was eventually shot dead in his home; *Col piremo*, they did strike.

Frankie Yale returned to New York where he would be the head of the Sicilian mob. Unfortunately, he double-crossed "Big Al" who stayed in Chicago, and was machine-gunned as he drove home. His car crashed into the brick steps of a neighbor's house.

Many of my family were not merely bystanders. They were blood related. They drank wine and danced with killers. They exchanged holiday gifts with assassins. They served as groomsmen and bridesmaids in the weddings of gangsters. And all of this, the social events and the church rituals, was done in an air of civility.

There was a strict dichotomy between a mobster's family life and their "business," (*affari*) which no one talked about openly, at least not until my mother talked to me during our cemetery visits.

She and my grandparents were witnesses, and more, far more.

As my mother approached age eighty, her short-term memory faltered. She would tell me a story she had told me in detail the day before. But her memories of events 60 and 70 years in the past were vivid, with exact details. The details had come from my grandfather Guglielmo and my Mom when she was the witness herself.

My mother Rosa would describe the apartments and the homes of the Genna brothers down to the color of the drapes, the sofas and the type of floor, even the view from the living room windows. Unless she had been there how else could my mother know such details?

While the *Terrible Genna brothers* and other notorious mobsters came to my grandfather's barbershop on Harrison, he was alternately summoned to Capone's Cicero headquarters at the Hawthorne Hotel and his Chicago headquarters at the Lexington Hotel for his barbering skills. Only the most trusted were allowed to shave Al with a straight razor.

One day in her early seventies I took my mother to the old McCormick Place to see a musical, she said, "This is where the Lexington Hotel was. That's where Capone had his headquarters. There was gold trim around the elevators and his 'friends' in the lobby checked every person who entered the elevator. Those who saw Capone got off at the fourth floor and went to room #430. It was a kind of reception area." My mother said calmly, "If your name was in the book you'd enter his six-room suite. It was beautiful, with beautiful Italian silk furniture, lamps with embroidered shades and fringe. The floor had big initials A and C in oak. It was parquet."

Of course there are numerous black and white photos of Al Capone from the newspapers of the period reprinted in history books. He was popular with the press like a folk hero and actually enjoyed interviews and having his photo taken, but there were no photos of his offices.

One day Mom took me to Capone's grave at Mt. Carmel Cemetery. It was only a stone's throw from the Genna's mausoleum. I looked for a mausoleum but there was only flat ground with heavy shrubbery. She knew exactly where he was buried, marked by a small headstone flush with the ground, covered by dirt and half sinking. There were large shrubs around a larger monument that had the name CAPONE running horizontally, the shrubbery intentionally covering the name. As usual, Mom made the sign of the cross and kissed her fingers saying, *"Buon' anima* (Rest his soul)." Beside his grave were other members of his family, including brothers Frank (killed in a shootout) and Ralph.

As we approached, a black Lincoln slowly drove away, "Wait," she said. On his headstone was the inscription "My Jesus Mercy." Someone had just placed a shiny nickel on the stone. My mother commented, "for good luck." Then she remarked, "This is not where he was buried the first time." I had never read that in any history of the Mafia.

"Did you ever visit that grave?" I asked her. "Of course," she replied.

Mom continued, "It was a cemetery in the city (Chicago). They had a very large stone house like a cave, but the family was afraid someone might put graffiti on it or steal his body. They brought his casket here and moved the other members of the family at night."

Reporters and rival gang members had always predicted that a bullet would end Capone's life. But such was not the case. Capone once said, "Once you are in, there is no out." There is no retirement from the mob. You do not betray the code of silence, *omerta*.

Capone went to prison in 1931. President Hoover had a law changed that created a loophole that would snare Capone. Illegal profits had to be taxed, the law stated, and so they got Capone on income tax evasion. He was never prosecuted for one murder, even though he was responsible for hundreds. He went to the Atlanta penitentiary and then to "The Rock," Alcatraz Island. Beyond going "stir crazy" at Alcatraz, he suffered from untreated syphilis and a softening of the brain called *paresis*. In 1939 he was released for good behavior. By then the disease had taken its toll. He had lost considerable weight, had crinkled skin, was bald and talked gibberish. One former associate, Frank Rio, watched him stare vacantly at the ceiling. He lived his last days, until his death in 1947, at his Miami estate, not knowing who he was or the power he once wielded.

In the end, Capone had no large funeral. Tony Accardo who inherited the leadership of the Chicago mob, ordered other mob members to stay away from the funeral because the "heat is on." The feds were taking down names and license plate numbers. Capone had no marble mausoleum, but he outlived his enemies and died in bed and not by a bullet.

What surprised me most was Mom's physical description of the mobster (Capone); more detailed than what an old black and white photo would reveal. They were the kind of details you only get from someone who had stood next to Capone himself. He was relatively short at 5 feet 8 inches. He weighed 190 pounds, but by 1929 he would gain an additional 35 pounds. Many had seen the prominent scar on his left cheek running to his chin, giving him the nickname "Scarface." Mom once told me "he had a large head, a short neck, and very black and bushy eyebrows."

We know from photos that Capone often wore a broad rimmed fedora hat and long black overcoat with velvet trim at the collar in Chicago and white suits and light straw hats in Florida. He smoked cigars constantly and had over 150 fine tailored suits.

Al would sit and listen to Italian ballads and opera that would bring him to tears. Mom had sung and performed ballads and opera for the Genna brothers. Did she ever sing for Capone? At his headquarters? Or party house?

Later in life Mom did not see the purpose of holding the secrets of her youth. One day, she said as we sat on a wood swing at my Wheaton home, "Capone's fingers were very short and stubby, but they looked strong." Another time when I brought her to the Allerton Hotel on Michigan Avenue for lunch, she talked about the parties on the top floor (20th) called the "Tip Top Room." It was 1973 and the room looked the same as it did 43 years earlier. (Today the room is a Holiday Inn health club.) "This is where Capone's sister Mafalda had an engagement party," she told me. Was my mother present?

Mom was fond of jewelry and although my father had pawned most of her really good jewelry, she had an eye for quality. She commented, "You should have seen his (Al Capone's) ring, a huge diamond (11.5 carats). It cost $50,000 in 1930." Then she added, "That was before taxes and after the crash (the stock market fall)," adding, "He wore it on his middle finger, right hand." She also commented on a large diamond belt buckle. I have looked at over 30 photos of Capone from that era and never saw the buckle.

My grandfather enjoyed having his photo taken. He especially liked portraits dressed in his best suit with a vest, a pocket watch and fob, spats and even a pearl cane. Like those he associated with, showing off your wealth was considered important.

In Italian he told his daughter Rosa, "*Pochi lo videro*," (few people saw him, referring to Capone) implying he was one of the *select*, to visit gangster royalty.

Al Capone always had a hand in his pocket when he had his photo taken, which was usually as he was moving from hotel door to waiting car. Mom said that was because "his hand was touching his automatic." But this next observation most likely came from someone who would get

as close as a barber. My grandfather would say, *"Ho visto una pistola piccola nella sun tasca di maglia"* (Sometimes I saw a small gun in his vest pocket) to his daughter
To my knowledge, Al Capone was never in my house. But many of his mob, his most ruthless hit men and a duo called the "homicide squad," were frequent guests, as well as his brothers, Ralph and Frank.

Capone was 21 years old when he was brought from New York to Chicago in 1920. He had worked in back room gambling parlors, brothels, and bars making $50 a week. When Johnny Torrio, the former leader of his juvenile gang in New York, turned over the rackets in Chicago to Capone, he never envisioned what Capone would do with a crime business turned into a vice empire.

The temperance movement in turn of the century America detested drunkenness, especially among the German, Irish and Italian immigrants who filled large cities. Their attempt to legalize morality became the 18th Amendment to the Constitution which prohibited the production and selling of alcohol. Little did Congress suspect they created a vast mob empire in America by giving them a large financial boost.

Capone would have stayed with petty gambling and prostitution but was smart enough to realize the European immigrants liked drinking Chianti in Italian homes, beer in German beer halls, and whiskey in Irish pubs. They were not about to stop, laws or not. From a business perspective it was simply a question of supply and demand.

To understand Capone's empire, it is important to translate the money of the 1920s into today's economy. Consider this, Al Capone in his early twenties was making $70 million a year on the sale of illegal alcohol and $105 million a year on his other rackets that included gambling, prostitution and kickbacks. In nine years, Al Capone was making $300 million a year by 1929. By today's economy, that would be 3.03 billion dollars a year. He is still considered the richest outlaw in world history.

Those years have become part of American folklore. Like
Tombstone and the gunfight at the O.K. Corral, the
gangsters of the *Roaring Twenties* have become woven into
the fabric of our country's restless growing pains, just like
the *Wild West*. They are legend, but were also real.

Capone's office was a suite of rooms at the Hawthorne
Hotel in Cicero (his home was at 7244 Prairie Avenue on the
south side of Chicago). He spent so much time at his office
he would often not go home until weekends, although he
had a strong affection for his mother, wife and son. Capone
did much of his business in his dressing gown and slippers.
Al had lavish athletic facilities: a full size gym, a handball
court, punching bags and a rowing machine. In his late 20s
he was more fond of pasta so did not use the exercise
machines himself. They were primarily for his bodyguards;
his 14 top men called torpedoes (*siluri*) that surrounded him
whenever he moved. He had more bodyguards than
President Hoover.

One of his top assassins was Jack McGurn. This was
certainly not an Italian name. Mom told me, "He changed
his name. He's an Italian from the old country. His real
name is DeMora," Mom said matter-of-fact. My mother
was good with names.

Jack DeMora had changed his name to McGurn when he
became a professional boxer. One day, his father was killed
in an early gangland war in Chicago, and he swore revenge.
Most of what he did for Capone by sending people to the
morgue was done out of a spirit of vengeance and
retaliation for his father's death.

Jack's nickname was "Machinegun McGurn" because that
was the only weapon he used. In the 1920s it was not
illegal to own a machinegun, a weapon developed for use
in World War I. It became the favored weapon of the
Chicago gangs. The weapon's nickname was "the Chicago
piano" for the RAT-TAT-TAT sound. The Thompson
submachine gun (.45 caliber) would hold either a round
cylinder with 100 rounds or a regular "stick looking"

magazine holding 20-30 rounds. Capone required Jack to workout in his gym everyday and Jack, by nature, favored the punching bag. Big Al wanted the men closest to him to be in top shape.

Behind the myths are reality. No need to exaggerate their violence and ruthlessness, it was very real. These were men without guilt, remorse, or conscience.

Capone never wore a bulletproof vest for several reasons. In the 1920s they were big and bulky, and he did not like the vest making him look even heavier. Another reason was that Sicilian hired guns (*assassino*) always shot their victims in the head. But probably a third reason was that he trusted the men who were closest to him. One key bodyguard was Frank Rio. He was always a few steps away from Big Al or in an adjacent room. When Hymie Weiss shot up the Hawthorne Café in retaliation for the killing of O'Banion, it was Frank that jumped on Al and covered his body, saving his life.

One evening in Philadelphia Al and Frank were coming out of a movie theater. Police surrounded them, discovered concealed weapons, and Al Capone was convicted of having a concealed weapon and received a one-year prison sentence in Pennsylvania. Rio, with the identical charge, received the exact same term, went to the same prison, and became a cellmate of Al, serving time with him. I never read it in a crime history book, but my family knew that Al and Frank wanted to be caught. It was a setup with the police. That may sound strange but after the St. Valentine's Day Massacre, there was a mob meeting on the east coast to discuss the ramifications and the heat from the feds. There was a type of United Nations developing with the gangs of New York and Chicago where different ethnic groups would work together. This would include the Jews, the Germans, the Irish and the Italians. It was simply good for business that people of different European ancestry work together for the cause of a crime syndicate. Powerful families in New York were frightened that the federal government would step in and crush their businesses. The

St. Valentine's Day Massacre had made international news.
New York *families* did not like the attention. My family
knew that at this private meeting Big Al accepted a
punishment. *"Accettare una punizione"* my grandfather said
to his daughter. He was willing to go to prison for a year,
not in Chicago but in Pennsylvania where the Philadelphia
mob would look out for him in prison where the guards
and the warden were on the "take." Capone did not have a
traditional cell. He had a carpet, plush chairs, wore his
slippers and dressing gown, and ate his favorite Italian
meals brought to him by his bodyguard Frank. Al would
listen to opera on his record player to pass the time.
Unlimited phone calls were another privilege. He ran his
Chicago mob from his cell.

Obviously, prison officials and guards were well
compensated to allow their "special" prisoner the *comforts of
home.* No such arrangement could work on such a grand
scale today, although mob "family" that have gone to
prison in recent years have had extensive privileges. One
can still compensate a guard, put money in his bank
account or buy furs and jewels for the guard's wife. Only
someone naïve would say, "That's impossible."

My mother also told me, "Capone had a deep gravely voice
with an Italian New York accent." (The newsreel films of
the 1920s had no sound.) She also commented that he had a
"broad smile and perfect teeth." Not exactly the portrait of
a vicious killer.

When he made an agreement on a shipment of illegal
liquor, he never put anything in writing. His word was his
bond along with his handshake. If you violated the terms,
no need to worry about a lawsuit. Consequences were
swift and certain.

Apparently Capone commanded tremendous loyalty from
those around him. His enemies offered thousands upon
thousands of dollars to kill him and yet his staff protected
him and with few exceptions, could not be bought.

A popular crime reporter for the Chicago Tribune, Jake Lingle, once wrote in a column, "The police commissioner is gathering evidence on Capone." It was more than a story; it was actually a tip. Capone decided upon reading the morning newspaper to visit the Police Commissioner John Stege immediately.

It wasn't just a ride; it was a motorcade. Capone exited the Lexington Hotel on Lake Shore Drive with Rio steps behind and 14 bodyguards. By gang ranking, they were all lieutenants in his army. The trip to the loop took ten-minutes. Capone rode in his $20,000, 7-ton armor-plated car with bulletproofed windows. In front were several lead cars and behind were several more cars for a total of seven cars and men heavily armed with "tommy" guns. The only things missing were the motorcycles beside him and flags on the hood of a visiting dignitary. No police dared stop him and his armed bodyguards from entering Chicago Police Headquarters. (Most were on his payroll anyway.) Without hesitating at the secretary's desk, Capone bolted into the commissioner's office. Several reporters followed. The police commissioner stood to attention, shocked. It was a showdown.

"Show me your evidence!" the steely-eyed Capone said to the police commissioner.

"We have none," Stege said sheepishly. They never had any evidence on Capone. Then Police Commissioner John Stege and Al Capone posed for pictures, and Capone left police headquarters as quickly as he had arrived. He commented to one reporter before stepping into his huge black sedan, "They've hung everything on me, but the Chicago Fire." The reporters laughed.

Dion O'Banion, the Irish leader of the North Side Gang, was infringing on Big Al's territory and cutting into his profits with whiskey and beer sales. It was obvious he had to be eliminated. When O'Banion was not out killing people, he loved working with flowers. He owned a flower shop directly across from the Holy Name Cathedral. "Deannie" had served there as an altar boy and sang in the choir. Many said he had a fine Irish tenor voice. He also was a patron of opera. His wife, of course, saw him as a comical, refined and gentle man. Yet, he had personally killed over 200 men, and kept Capone and the Genna brothers out of the north side with their alcohol.

Cardinal Mundelien, a prince of the church dressed in royal robes and pulling a long red train, celebrated mass in the cathedral where Dion was a faithful attender. Kneeling at the altar rail, receiving communion from the Cardinal and bowing his head in fervent prayer, he appeared honest and devout.

Capone's hits were never ruthless or sloppy but well planned. He would never engage in a simple drive-by, taking the chance of missing his intended victim. Every murder was tailored to the weakness of the victim. His men studied the victim's patterns.

Mike Merlo was head of the Sicilian Union (Unione Siciliano). My grandfather belonged to the union, which had regular meetings on Taylor Street in Chicago's Little Italy. One had to be full-blooded Sicilian to be a member and even born in Sicily to become the president of the union so my grandfather was eligible. These "Sons of Sicily" were a front for the production of illegal gin, bourbon and scotch. My grandfather played a role in this business. Being born in Brooklyn and his parents coming from Naples, Capone was never eligible to be a member or the president of the union, and this was always a sore spot for him. This powerful union controlled most of the production of the illegal alcohol in Chicago that Capone sold.

O'Banion detested Capone but not for business reasons. As strange as it sounds, he had a warped sense of morality. Gambling and bootlegging were okay, but he strongly disapproved of prostitution, which after all, was how Capone got his start. Along with Big Jim Colosimo, Capone controlled almost all the whorehouses in Chicago. Dion thought that was immoral.

One day Mike Merlo mysteriously died, reportedly ill. This was really a part of the plot to get Dion O'Banion. A phone call was placed to his florist shop.

"Big Al wants a large floral tribute," the voice said. "We'll send Alberto and John to pick it up this afternoon." O'Banion agreed. The order actually appealed to his pride. The Sicilian mob funerals were a big event in Little Italy. The visitation sometimes went on for three days with as many as 40,000 people filing past the open casket. Big Al always sent the largest floral bouquet and, in addition, would purchase several carloads of flowers. This would bring O'Banion thousands of dollars for one funeral. Since everyone would look at Big Al's giant wreaths, Dion would be showing his florist skills to the public and the press, which O'Banion could not resist.

O'Banion had a tough side, too, and always carried three guns; one in each coat pocket and one in an ankle holster. He was finishing the Merlo wreath and had removed his coat. He had placed one of the smaller guns in his vest pocket. O'Banion's Florist Shop was a two-storied brick building with a large striped awning. It said "Schofield Company" above the awning and a large neon sign suspended from the top floor had one word "flowers." It was a "front" for O'Banion's illegal beer business. He had placed his liquor in saloons in Cicero telling Capone that he only made $20,000 a month. Capone learned he was making $100,000 a month with no cut to Capone, a bad move.

My mother heard the "homicide squad," John and Alberto, refer to the Irish gang leader as *Il Nemico* (The Enemy).

A black Ford touring car slowly rolled to the front of the florist shop. One passenger slipped down an alley and would come through a back door. As Scalise and Anselmi got out of the car they glanced at the large, open oak doors of the cathedral. They had both been in the cathedral many times for weddings and gangland funerals. Both men pretended to worship, kneeling with black hearts and no conscience. John Scalise and Alberto Anselmi entered the florist shop with smiles that hid the fact they were notorious killers from Sicily dubbed "the homicide squad," O'Banion did not know their past. They had come *"heavy"*, carrying loaded guns.

This was the first of the "glad hand" or "Sicilian handshake" murders. O'Banion was holding a pruning tool in his left hand when he shook hands with Scalise. The killer grabbed his hand and his wrist with a firm grip as Anselmi grabbed his other hand, also with a firm grip to his wrist, saying, *"E' sui punto di morire.* (He is about to die.)" As they kept his hands from reaching for the gun in his vest pocket, Frankie Aiello (brought in from New York) shot O'Banion in the back of the head with a .22. They were still holding Dion's wrists as his body went limp and crumpled to the floor. All three shot him several more times. O'Banion was quoted as saying, "All Sicilians can go to hell," before Aiello fired. My grandfather heard the details in his basement from John and Alberto over wine. *"Sparare a morte* (Gunned down)," John said with a smirk and a nod, his glass eye glistening.

My grandparents and mother attended the funeral more out of a sense of spectacle than of sadness. Up until 1924, this was the largest funeral in the history of Chicago. Moral people were disgusted, but the community at large was intrigued. The Chicago Symphony Orchestra played at the funeral in the armory. The funeral cortege was a mile long with twenty-six cars filled with flowers. The Chicago Cardinal refused a service in the Cathedral or burial in the Catholic cemetery, which was considered consecrated ground. Roman Catholic canon law prohibits burial of public criminals who had "no sign of repentance," but O'Banion was buried near the tomb of the bishops anyway.

No expense was spared. He was buried in three coffins, one of bronze, one of silver, and one of lead. A window looked down on his reconstructed face and his right hand rested on a purple velvet pillow, his gun hand. A priest came to say prayers at the graveside where there were 10,000 spectators including my grandparents. O'Banion's wife was overcome with emotion, repeatedly screaming, "Why would they do this?" She did not have a clue about his double identity. Of course, the Gennas and Al Capone attended the funeral, too, to pay their respects and pretend to mourn for the police and press. Angelo Genna winked at my grandfather, Guglielmo.

A Jewish mobster, Hymie Weiss, was the second in command under O'Banion, and he quickly took over the North Side mob using the florist shop as his headquarters. Weiss knew that Capone was behind the killing and said, "A bullet is going to put the Big Shot in his marble mausoleum."

He did not have a carefully thought out plan, simply a show of impetuous force. He and 24 men in 12 cars headed for Cicero days after O'Banion's funeral. Twelve black cars each containing two men holding machineguns made their way to the Hawthorne Hotel in broad daylight. Someone had tipped off Weiss that Capone was eating in the café, which had large glass windows looking out to the street. Seeing the dark parade, police got out of their way. This was before the age of helicopters and sophisticated roadblocks. A Chicago *copper* (named after his copper badge) was not paid enough to die in gangland crossfire.

As all 12 cars rounded a corner, they slowly lined up in front of the café. 24 machine guns pointing out of the car windows began shooting. The sound was deafening. As a hail of bullets flew, there was the sound of shattering glass, the loud pops of the punctured tires of 38 parked cars and wood of the restaurant tables splintering. Over 1,000 rounds were shot into the café in 30 seconds.

With Capone was one bodyguard, Frank Rio, who threw Capone to the floor. Thirty-eight automobiles on the street were riddled with holes, but Capone was unharmed and soon increased his security.

Next, a rival gang member went to the chef of the restaurant and tried to pay him to poison Capone's minestrone soup with puric acid. The chef wasn't stupid. He immediately told Capone, who braced himself for a fierce gangland war in Chicago. With 1,000 gunmen, he had the strongest mob gang in town.

Did Weise not think Capone would get revenge? Being a "good" Catholic, many Italians thought it was a miracle that St. Genaro, the patron saint of Naples, had saved the life of Capone. Everyone waited for retaliation, but days and weeks went by and nothing happened. Capone was not as impulsive as Weiss. He was not going to send carloads of hit men.

Capone's men diligently staked out Hymie's inherited flower shop. There was an alley, a side door, a back door and a front door. One of Capone's lieutenants rented a room at 740 N. State specifically asking the landlord for a room on the second floor overlooking the street. From his window he had a view of the front of the shop and the side entrance off the alley. The same week, an unknown woman went to One West Superior Street and rented an apartment specifying the second floor at the rear of the building, which had a view of the rear door of the florist shop.

Hymie Weiss came and went, yet nothing happened. He felt safe. He always kept a bodyguard close at hand. In the room on Superior and the room on State Street there were three men in each. The six men had brought "violin cases" (actually large black cases mistaken for instrument cases) that contained machine guns into the building. They were in no hurry. Day after day these *assassino* (hired killers) would anxiously smoke cigarettes, peer out the windows and eat sandwiches brought to them by the woman. Frequently, Weiss would pass under the muzzles hidden in the shadows of the apartments, but they waited.

Then one day the moment came. Hymie Weiss' car pulled into the alley. As he stepped from his car, six men, three in each window, leaned forward and six machine guns spewed hot lead. The echoes from the alley reverberated up the aisle of the cathedral across the street. Hymie fell, hit by ten bullets. His driver, Peller, was hit twice. A politician named Jacobs was hit by two bullets. Hymie's lawyer, O'Bryan, was hit by three bullets, and Hymie's bodyguard, Murray, was hit by seven bullets. No one survived.

There were no witnesses. When the police examined each room, all they found were three chairs and a pile of cigarette butts. The North Side Gang had lost their new boss. One of O'Banion's fiercest hit men, Louis Alterie, who always wore three guns like O'Banion himself and had once been a cowboy, promptly left Chicago, went back West, never to return. His connections (police) helped him get out of town.

What does it mean to have "connections?" Basically, it means the ability to get things done. Connections kept the police from investigating O'Banion's killing and the hit on Weiss, due to Capone's influence.

When we relate this term to a crime family, it implies very bad ethics. This is how godfathers like Joseph Bonanno and John Gotti weaved their way around the system. This is how Capone and the Genna brothers were able to have so much financial success.

Having connections means knowing people in high places, people who can get things done by looking the other way. You might own a "legitimate" construction company (in terms of the ability to build a highway, a bridge or an office building), but how you get your materials and how you even get the job, well, that's another matter.

Sometimes the connections would be involved in "bid rigging." You would get the job by getting inside information and adjusting your bid accordingly. That was a different era, of course. Back in the 1920s and 30s, and even up until the 1950s, traffic tickets were not logged into computers. Jury members were reachable. Judges could be influenced. Officials could be bribed and "bought." It's not that it doesn't still happen, it's just that prosecutors and police are more cautious and aware today.

My family had connections and I was related to their sphere of immoral influence.

And when you helped the *family*, they were always appreciative. They were always grateful and would return a favor with a favor. Their generosity might include an expensive pen, imported leather gloves, a case of wine or a new set of tires. A judge, an alderman, a mayor, or a chief of police, often received presents even when it wasn't Christmas. Only they knew the relationship between the gift and their services.

We think in terms of good guys and bad guys. In Cagney movies police won and gangsters lost (died).

The mob, especially during the Capone era, made it hard to tell who were good and who were bad. Italians knew them as *"famiglia* (family)." Capone created soup kitchens for the needy. Mobsters were generous with each other, good husbands and great dads. Rivals were bad because they hurt business or killed family.

But in real life, the authority figures were equally bad. The aldermen played cards with the mob. The judges and police captains were on the "take." Elections were bought and stolen. Without the "respectable" people, organized crime would not flourish.

So, who were the good guys?

Large churches were built with mafia money. The priests and bishops knew it. They took the money without a blink or a hesitation. Cardinal Mundelein built a small model of Rome, including a man made lake and a mansion with fine art and gold plumbing. His elegant downtown residence with a fleet of limousines was built in 1925. Was it a coincidence this was the leader of the Chicago Catholic Church in the Capone era or that all the dominant gang leaders, the German (Moran), Irish (O'Banion), and Italian (Capone), were Catholic?

My family knew mayors and congressmen on the take. Priests my family knew played cards and bet on the "ponies" alongside crime figures.

Who were the good guys? To my family, the answers were simple: those that didn't get caught, those that became wealthy, and those who died of natural causes.

Even Capone paid reporters to get positive press, but one reporter did business with a rival gang member which concerned Big Al.

Capone was always anxious to get press. He liked reading about himself. The most popular crime reporter of the day was Jake Lingle. He worked for the *Chicago Tribune*. The creator and publisher of the mighty *Chicago Tribune* was Colonel McCormick. He fought in World War I, and was a conservative republican who supported prohibition. Of course, his large mansion in West Chicago, some 35 miles west of the city, had a secret door that revealed a well-stocked bar for his private guests and family, not uncommon.

Lingle kept Capone in the papers. That was Capone's connection to the press. He lived at the Stevens Hotel and on June 9, 1930, he walked to his office at the Tribune Building on Michigan Avenue beside the Chicago River. After making a few phone calls, he walked over to the Sherman House in the Loop where he often had lunch. It was a hot day. He thought at least two men were trailing him, so he told a police sergeant in the lobby of the Sherman Hotel, but the sergeant did not see anyone. Jack was headed for a train to the Washington Park Racetrack, as he enjoyed gambling. He walked past Grant Park, then up

Randolph, and entered the subway at the library. The platform was crowded and unbeknownst to him, two drivers waited in cars on the street level. Four men surrounded him on the platform with two additional men at each exit. A hand came out of the crowd; there was a single shot to the back of his head. When Lingle fell, his cigar was still in his mouth and his hand still clutched his racing form.

Colonel McCormick was furious. He pounded his desk with a closed fist and insisted that no expense be spared investigating the death of one of his star reporters. Investigations did not reveal what McCormick wanted to know, however. Lingle was on Capone's payroll. He made $65 a week as a reporter but spent $65,000 a year. He played the stock market with Police Commissioner, William Russell, and had heavy losses from the1929 crash. He had invested $25,000 to fix dog races that would be run at the Chicago Stadium, borrowing the money from one of Moran's gang members, Jack Zuta.

Unfortunately for Lingle, the courts blocked the dog racing and he had already spent most of his money. He then went to Joe Aiello to create a gambling room at the Biltmore Athletic Club. A police raid (the commissioner did not have time to block) ended that plan.

Zuta wanted his money from Lingle immediately. The day before, a black sedan followed him as he walked from the Tribune Building to the Sherman House. Nothing happened. It was simply a warning of impending doom. Neither the police commissioner nor Capone had any interest in ending Lingle's life. Capone sent some of his men to a summer resort in Wisconsin where one of Zuta's men was listening to a music box when machine guns riddled him. Joe Aiello, another of Lingle's assassins, was nervous and scared and was hiding in an apartment building waiting for the right time to take a train out of the city.

Rose Huebsch worked for the state's attorney's office and recognized Zuta in an apartment across the hall. Capone decided to turn him over to the police commissioner. They arranged a telephone call. The telephone was in the hall. They awoke Zuta who came out in a robe and slippers and promptly arrested him. Capone did not have to kill Zuta. Behind a massive black metal door at the old Division One of Cook County Jail on California Avenue, Jack Zuta had an appointment with the electric chair for Lingle's death.

Today connections are more sophisticated in the business world. It might be a pharmaceutical company giving a golf outing or a vacation package to a physician with a two-hour educational lecture at Hilton Head or another fine resort area. Junkets are the modern day bribery of politicians. I have been to large justice conferences where state officials attended one 90-minute session then headed out to the golf course for the next three days. The average taxpayer doesn't know this, of course. It's really the same thing that organized crime has done with officials for over 80 years. It just looks more sophisticated today.

The most common "thank you" gift I remember that my godfather and uncles gave to officials was a new wristwatch. I don't know where the wristwatches came from, but they seemed to have a large supply in bulk.

Now that is the pleasant part of connections: giving favors in return for a favor. But what happened when you were assured of something and you were double-crossed? That was another matter. There was retaliation for the jockey who failed to hold back his horse, for the boxer who did not take a dive, and for the ball player who did not strike out. Any contest, usually a sports event where the family placed large bets and considered it a "sure thing," would have dire consequences when the person who was paid off failed to follow through.

The best that one could hope for would be an "accident." They would be lucky if the only retaliation was a broken leg or an arm that would be in a cast for six weeks.

If there was a major transgression, a person would "disappear." That is to say, "meet their maker" or be "pushing up daisies on a farm in northern Indian," a favorite mob burial ground for enemies.

Only when the mob wanted to send a warning to other potential double-crossers, would the victim be found with evidence of torture before death to send a stern warning.

Those who carried out the retaliation, the hit men, the paid assassins, did they enjoy killing? Not really. They were dispassionate about their work. It was simply a "job." It was something you had to do. They were emotionless and did not see a person as a victim but rather an object or a target.

And if the victim appealed to their humanity or asked for mercy, well, they never got it. The assassins had cold hearts. As my grandmother, Santa, would say, "*Cuori freddi*". They acted like atheists at the core, but hoped for some last minute mercy from God for the prayers they said as children, serving as an altar boy.

My "uncles" wore gold crosses. My father had a holy card in his wallet. Mobsters genuflected in church. But it was all merely superstition.

That was perhaps the biggest gamble of all. They assumed they could live a life of crime and depravity without fearing God. The biggest gamble mob members ever made was not on a football game or a horserace. The biggest gamble was with their immortal soul.

As the Sicilians would say about evil people, "*Vomitare l'anima.* (They threw up their soul)." Mom once said to me walking past Mob graves, "*Salutare l'un l'altro nell' inferno*" (they will greet each other in hell).

I was invisible

I was invisible.

I was invisible to my father, it seemed to me.

I do not mean I could not be seen like *The Invisible Man* story or motion picture. I have met many young people who were not with their fathers because of divorce, or their mother got pregnant and was abandoned. There is another type of invisibility.

With all my family's *connections*, I was not connected to my father.

Although my father stayed married to my mother for thirty-five years and we shared the same house, he was emotionally distant to me. Physically, he was hardly there because of his card games and racetrack gambling.

What I mean by being invisible is that I was not given the attention, the affirmation or the love I needed. I interpreted his actions as rejection. I assumed I was not worthy of his attention.

In my early twenties, I "ran away" to a Benedictine monastery in western Missouri. I was a Roman Catholic, ordained in the Church, living the life of a monastic cleric in a large basilica and abbey. At the time, I thought of myself as a very religious person, but now I realize much was playacting.

My key motive for becoming a priest was to serve God. But I became so involved in my outward appearance, what a cleric wears and the rituals performed, that I really thought I could work my way to heaven by being a good person. I also thought my good works would *save* my family, especially the criminal ones.

I also remember thinking that since my family did not go to church, and my father really gave no indication as to whether or not he even believed in God, if I did something good with my life, I could get all of them into heaven. I meant well.

Now that I am older, I realize I was also running away from home. Not in the way teenagers run away from home, but hiding, to be sure. Hiding from what? The yelling, the screaming, the constant tension, and my ulcer, all led me to seek a place of peace. And a monastery is a peaceful, tranquil place. I made myself invisible from my family.

But even in such a place, I learned about the church's connection to the Chicago mob, connections largely hidden from the public.

A bishop who as a priest was a close assistant of Cardinal Mundelein's told me stories one evening. He was visiting the monastery from outside Chicago. The assistant priest to the cardinal, now a bishop, was a friend. We had a bar in the seminary and many of the priests and bishops were heavy drinkers. It was late in the evening and the bishop had a lot to drink and became very talkative. He described the inside of the Mundelein mansion. "It had gold plated plumbing. Not just the faucets but behind the walls...there were so many paintings by Renaissance artists that the archdiocese could go bankrupt and live off the sales for ten years," he said boldly with a broad smile, holding a glass of bourbon.

"Did the Cardinal know people?" I asked him, implying the Chicago mob.

"He knew everyone," the aged bishop replied.

I asked him about the O'Banion funeral which I knew of from my mother who had watched the somber parade on the street.

"Mundelein did not want O'Banion to be buried in Mt. Carmel," the bishop told me. "He (Cardinal) put his foot down. He said no. No priest was to give the rites!" (A priest from the cathedral could have walked across the street to give O'Banion the last rites, but no one came.) "There was no church mass and no burial in consecrated ground," the bishop continued. "Of course, Malloy defied him and the cardinal was furious. I saw him slam the phone down when he heard Malloy had gone to the gravesite."

"Who was Malloy?" I asked.

"That S. O. B. friend of O'Banion!" the bishop replied, slightly slurring his speech.

He went on to explain that Father Malloy was raised with O'Banion in a section of town called "Little Hell." By the bishop's tone and expressions it was obvious that Father Malloy was very familiar with the mob. In fact, according to the Bishop, he was equally at ease with Moran, O'Banion and Capone, rivals and enemies. Malloy went to O'Banion's gravesite and said prayers. This was witnessed by thousands of mourners including my grandparents.

Three years earlier Cardinal Mundelein moved to Chicago from Brooklyn. His predecessor had built a tremendous mausoleum on a hill in Mt. Carmel cemetery. There were large bronze statues, Corinthian columns and Romanesque architecture in this mausoleum. Although closed to the public, I have been inside and gazed at the 40 by 30 foot mosaic images in gold and the white marble statues. All the bishops and cardinals are buried there, but one.

Cardinal Mundelein is the only prelate of the Catholic archdiocese not buried in the ornate tomb. He chose instead his own estate. A dozen of the fiercest mobsters in Chicago are in close proximity to the bishop's tomb and hundreds more including Sam Giancana are buried in that cemetery.

The O'Banion gravesite had a gaudy, large monument that said "My Sweetheart" from his wife. The cardinal was very unhappy. Five months after O'Banion died, she bought a plot not more than 60 feet from the entrance to the bishop's tomb, literally facing the doors. By all accounts she moved closer to the Episcopal tomb out of spite, because "Deanie" was denied the final rites of the church. Mundelein was again furious and had the monument removed. But it was only replaced by a larger blank obelisk, which remains today.

"Whatever happened to Malloy?" I asked.

"Now that's interesting," he laughed, downing another drink, "Father Malloy became a bag man. (Someone who delivers mob payments.) He was going between Moran and Capone until money disappeared ... about $600,000 was 'misplaced,'" the bishop smiled.

The cardinal received a gruff phone call from one of Capone's men. "Get rid of Malloy by midnight or he will be at the bottom of the Chicago River!"

The next day Mundelein transferred the priest to Argentina. Malloy lived there, Rome, and other cities in Europe with a rather lavish lifestyle until he finally came back to Chicago in the 1950s. He was elevated to a new church position by Chicago Cardinal Stritch and had a welcome home party with Mayor Daley and members of the mob attending. "Who says crime doesn't pay?" the bishop laughed.

He added one other story that only he could authenticate. Mundelein had died in the ornate church he had built in the miniature Rome with Sisters of Perpetual Adoration taking care of the church. According to his former assistant, "He had a heart attack. He was on the toilet at the time and fell over. We discovered his body and it was a mess. We had to clean him, change his clothes, put on his vestments, and dragged him into the church. We put out his chalice and draped his body on the altar." The bishop smiled from ear to ear.

The official version (on sacred cards) was the nuns discovered him slumped on the altar, apparently having had a heart attack as he raised the sacred host celebrating mass.

The bishop commented, "That wouldn't look good on a holy card, the toilet and all. We gave him a much better send off." He laughed deeply.

Even in this religious environment there were hypocrisy, cynicism and connections to crime figures.

My second year in the monastery was 1969. It was Good Friday, the day we commemorate the death of Jesus. One of the monks knocked on my door at 5 a.m. while still pitch dark. He told me I had a phone call. Phone calls at that hour are often bad news. I picked up the handset apprehensively.

My brother Anthony was pretty abrupt, "Dad's dead," he blurted. I didn't know what to say, or even ask how or where. He was not very consoling or even kind. "Get home!" was his next command. Without money for airfare and having been awakened out of sound sleep, there was no time to think about details. When I did not respond quickly, he shouted into the phone, "Get your butt here!" The reverent atmosphere of the Abbey was broken.

Welcome back to the world of my family, a stunning contrast. Something was not being said and I could only guess what it was. My oldest brother, Joseph, picked me up at the airport; we went straight to the house. In his words, "We have to pick out a suit for the casket." This was all new to me.

It was so strange to walk into the house I grew up in knowing that Dad had died there only seven hours earlier. Paramedics did try to resuscitate him in the ambulance and the emergency room, but his fatal heart attack was at home. The house was now quiet. My first strong impression was of the tracks in the carpet from the ambulance stretcher. Joseph and I went into the bedroom. Of course, the bed was unmade. Dad's false teeth were still in a glass by the bed stand. Then I saw something that struck me as ironic. His wristwatch was sitting on the top of his dresser, the second hand moving. I picked it up and put it to my ear. I could hear the tick, tick, tick. His watch was still running while his heart was not.

I did not know what to feel. I was stuck in the middle of opposite emotions. I was not really sad. Later that day, after my brothers picked out the casket, I was sitting at a counter in a small coffee shop with my brother Anthony. This would have been a great opportunity for a brother-to-brother, heart-to-heart talk. He said very little. I asked him as many questions as I could, "How had Dad been feeling?"

He responded, "Fine."

"Was he worried about anything?"

"No."

"Did he have any stress?"

"No."

"So things were okay?"

"Yes, just fine," Anthony responded, never turning his head, never looking at me or giving me eye contact. There was a big secret, but I would not learn it until after the funeral.

When I saw my father's body in the casket, again I did not know what to feel. Relatives had already arrived, including, to my surprise, many who were on the "banned list" of people we were not supposed to associate with. I knew they came for my mother and not really for my father.

I heard hushed conversation and whispered phrases, "*Il cavallo da corsa* (Horse racing)," and "*E' rimasto senza niente* (He was left with nothing)."

Late in the evening on the first day of the wake, I was thinking about something and started to cry. My mother immediately assumed that I finally connected with my grief. In reality, I was not thinking about his death. I was searching my memory for one time my father had said to me, "I love you." I was trying to remember one time when my father put his arm on my shoulder and said, "I'm proud you're my son," but I couldn't think of one such time.

At the end of the funeral ceremony I suddenly realized what I was feeling, and I felt slightly guilty. I was relieved. Yes, relieved that he was gone because now, at last, there would be an end to the yelling, the threats of physical hitting, the tension, the waving of guns, and the tight knots in my stomach. At last, I thought, our family would be free of the connections to bookies, people who fixed boxing matches and horse races, and mysterious "uncles" at card games.

I really thought we would become a "normal" family, and my brothers and I would have clean lives, lives of respectability, honesty and closeness. It was a fantasy.

I was putting far too much blame on my father. I was making the assumption that all the associations to people involved with notorious crime came through him alone. I underestimated the Sicilian traditions and how effectively my brothers had inherited a crime culture and lifestyle, perhaps even a family curse that went back to my grandfather.

I wasn't seeking a criminal life. I was a quiet child. During the time I served as a bartender to my father and his friends at the card table, I enjoyed the attention. For a few minutes as I walked through the haze of cigar smoke and handed each of the men their drinks, I was seen, I was acknowledged. I sometimes got a pat on the head, a pinch on the cheek and even a couple of bucks. It felt good to be "visible."

My mother's insistence that I go with my father to the racetrack was, in her thinking, a way to bring my Dad and I closer together. It was, of course, also a fantasy. My father was so involved in studying the racing form, calculating his bet and then (during the race) screaming at his horse to win, I was rendered invisible. I remember walking through the stands alone picking up the brightly colored losing tickets. Dad would forget to even ask me if I was hungry. I would see people eating hotdogs and drinking sodas, as he was steeped in the science of his compulsion.

The rides home were silent.

Invisible is the right word. It was as if my father could look right through me and not really see me. If it had not been for my mother, who worked hard at teaching me good values and talking about virtue, I would have easily turned to rebellion and teenage crime to get his attention.

I often thought about running away from home but never really took any steps in that direction, more out of fear of my father's retaliation if caught.

I often thought about taking his gun in the small metal box and shooting him to protect my mother from a fierce battle. But I was too mindful of the Ten Commandments and thought that I would go to hell for such a mortal sin. I did sometimes shoot him in my nightmares and fantasies, however.

When I left home for college and then to seminary, my anger toward my father became real. I often thought he was disappointed with me. Perhaps he did not want a third child.

Mom would say, "Your father loves you, he just can't say it or show it." This was always difficult to understand, a real enigma.

Dad praised my older brother Joseph who took up boxing for a time. Both Joseph and Anthony, like my father, played cards, smoked and drank. So I wondered if he was disappointed with me that I did not pursue boxing, did not like gambling, and did not smoke nor drink, things *real* men did.

Once in college, rebellion kicked in. I began drinking excessively. It was nothing for me to drink six beers in a row, eventually downing hard liquor like gin, vodka and bourbon. I remember driving back to my dorm one night and not knowing how I got there. The next morning, frightened, I checked the morning newspaper for any story about a pedestrian struck by a car during my blackout. It was stupid and foolish behavior, and I did not even know why I was drinking so much. I started smoking, too. Oddly, not cigarettes, but cigars. You are not supposed to smoke cigars back-to-back like cigarettes, but I did. I guess I was identifying with all my "uncles."

All of these actions were just symptoms. It is often hard to analyze yourself at the time because we tend to fool ourselves and make excuses for our behaviors. I know I did. I truly did not know why I was so angry or why I was drinking so much. It would be years before I became honest with myself.

The sanctuary of the peaceful setting of the monastery was only a temporary respite. My father was buried, and in Joseph's tradition of impulsive temperament, my oldest brother erupted with anger when I decided to wait and watch Dad's casket lowered into the ground rather than going directly home from the small cemetery chapel. My oldest brother was great at name-calling. Joseph exclaimed, "You're stupid," "You're odd," or "You're just crazy." My father did not call me names; he just ignored me. I'm not sure which was worse, but neither was good.

There were a lot of secrets in the family while I was living in the monastery. I had not seen my father for a long time and rarely talked with him by phone. So what was the family secret surrounding my father's death? He was in his early fifties, relatively young for an adult male's death.

Now that he was gone, my mother decided to begin sharing some of the secrets with me and it began with recent history, something that happened only a month before Dad's death.

I did not know it, but Mom had left my father. After over thirty-five years of a rocky relationship, she had enough. Apparently she was going to visit someone on the "black list" at a party and my brother Anthony had come to pick her up. My father, with his Sicilian temper, commanded her not to leave. My brother decided to defy him, which was highly unusual. Anthony was going to take her to the party anyway. According to my mother, Dad and Anthony got into a fight, a real physical fight, and my brother ended up knocking my father down and pinning him to the floor. I was not there to see it, but it must have been an emotional scene. My mother told me she was screaming and crying as

my father and brother were having a fistfight. My brother
Anthony won. They walked out with Dad still on the floor.

It must have been hard on Dad's pride as a former boxer
and longshoreman. He was not used to losing anything,
and now, getting older, it must have come as a blow. But
worse yet, Mom did not return home. She moved out and
was living with my brother. I'm not sure if my father
thought she was going to divorce him or ever return.
According to my mother, she was trying to teach him a
lesson that "enough was enough." The family later learned
from the autopsy that my father Matteo had had a series of
heart attacks. We discovered from co-workers that he
would suddenly blackout and fall to the ground at work
and also during the weeks she was gone. He never told
family.

Everything we know today about heart attacks fits the
pattern. He was a very heavy smoker and drinker, had
high stress levels, and the combination of the gambling, bad
marriage, the stress of my mother leaving him and the
fistfight with my brother was probably the perfect
chemistry for his fatal heart attack. She had moved back
that week, but the stress had already taken its toll.

There was even more. My mother told me my brother
Anthony had felt terrible about pinning my father to the
floor and had written him a letter of apology and mailed it.
But the letter was sitting in the mailbox, delivered eight
hours after Dad died. He never read it.

I have often wondered what affect that had on Anthony.
Unfortunately he never talked to me about anything
personal or anything deep, so I will never know. My
brothers had learned, as had many Sicilians like my father,
not to talk about what they were feeling, not to "show their
cards," to keep everything tightly locked inside.

After my father's funeral, I returned to the monastery. I
was invisible to my older brothers Joseph and Anthony, and

I would become restless in the church, too. I knew too much. My family knew the church was tainted, also.

The Roman Catholic Church looked very different to me from the inside. My mother never went to church but was fixated on statues of saints in our house, which she kissed and venerated. But her devotion did not prevent her from being cynical, even about the death of a pope.

Could the mob alter history? My family thought so. In 1979 a new Pope was elected. His name was Albino Luciano from Venice. Mom was excited about his "goodness" and told me he was "going to change the church." He was by all accounts a good and honest man. His passion was returning the church to focus on the poor. The ceremony of the installation of a Pope is ornate if not gaudy. The new Pope is carried on a chair held aloft by several men. He wears a platinum crown studded with jewels.

The new Pope took the name Pope John Paul I. He declined the formal ceremony, and was installed as the new Vicar of the Church during a simple mass instead. Many became nervous, especially the princes of the church, the Cardinals, many who had mob ties. They were not ready to put aside the pomp and the power of the Roman Catholic Church. Thirty-three days later, the Pope was found dead. His doctors said he had a heart attack although he had been in good health.

My mother said, "He was such a good man, too good. They killed him. (*hanno uccisp il papa*)" I knew her meaning exactly. Growing up, Mom would say, "The Pope is God on earth, or the closest to him." But as I got older, she added, "Even the Pope has enemies. There are bad people who don't care who you are. *E vero!* (It is true!)" Mob friends of our family in Cicero suspected an assassination.

The word was out that the new Pope (John Paul II) was going to order an investigation of the Vatican Bank. The bank was 3.5 billion dollars in the red, and there was talk of involvement with the mob. As a matter of fact, mob connections with the Vatican go back to World War II when Lucky Luciano (the New York mob) helped fund the resistance movement in Italy that led the way for the invasion of Sicily by the Allies through the Vatican Bank.

The Catholic Church had a way of looking the other way when receiving mob money. When I was younger, my father often slowed his auto as we passed Tony Accardo's mansion in River Forest. A large Roman Catholic Church not far away, the size of a cathedral and made from solid stone, was his parish. Did the priests know that mob money was funding the building project?

Bishop Paul Marcinkus was the President of the Vatican Bank when allegations surfaced. There had been strong rumors that he was involved with Roberto Calvi, President of the Banco Ambrosiano. The FBI went to question Marcinkus for laundering 47 million dollars of Nazi gold stolen from the Jews during the war, through the Vatican Bank.

Marcinkus was a large and powerful man but he wasn't from Europe, he was born in Cicero, Illinois, in 1922 during the Capone era. He quickly rose in the church and spent most of his career in Vatican politics. He appointed himself bodyguard to the Pope, and was always seen very close to him, although each Pope officially had Swiss Guards for protection.

He was seen leaving the Pope's residence and walking across a garden courtyard the night Pope John Paul I died.

As our family watched the Vatican state funeral on television, my brother Anthony commented, "You can put digitalis in someone's food or hot chocolate and make it look like a heart attack." A new Pope was elected. Allegations were terminated and Marcinkus was promoted to Archbishop. He continued to be very close to John Paul II and money was shuttled to the Polish Solidarity Union on his direction.

Years later, Roberto Calvi was found hanging from the Black Friar's Bridge in London. It was proclaimed a suicide although his hands were tied behind his back and heavy bricks were found in his pockets. There was 1.3 billion dollars missing from his bank, but it had made its way into the Vatican Bank.

Marcinkus remains under the protection of the Vatican today. Italian police wanted to interview him about several murders, but he lived as a "prisoner" in the Vatican for many years and only recently moved to Phoenix, Arizona, where he is still protected from interrogation because he holds a Vatican diplomatic passport.

My father's only comment to me when I left home for the seminary was, "They (priests and bishops) are human. They are just like us. They play politics, too."

Because my family never went to church, my attendance, especially visiting church daily after school, was invisible to them. I was trying hard to find a way to heaven surrounded by a jungle of crime and conspiracy.

But of all people in my life it was with my father that I most felt invisible.

We were strangers, my father and I. We lived under the same roof, but we did not know each other. He never tucked me in, said prayers with me, read a bedtime story, or held my hand when I was sick.

We were strangers. My father did not know what I thought or dreamed about. He didn't know who my friends were, the subjects I studied in school, my favorite color, my favorite foods, or my favorite movies.

My mother knew all of these, of course, because she listened to me. Food was her way of connecting. She delighted in cooking roasted chicken with oregano, lemon juice, and rosemary, Veal Parmesan and slices of prosciutto with radicchio leaves, olive oil, and fresh ground pepper, which were among my favorite foods. I would watch her cook. Together Mom and I celebrated eating. But my father and I rarely ate a meal together, so he wouldn't know what I liked or ate.

We were strangers, my father and I. He did not know me, nor did I know him. I wanted to know him, of course. I wanted to know what it was like for him to steam into New York Harbor and see the Statue of Liberty from the deck of the *Perugia*, but I never asked.

I wanted to know what it was like for him growing up in Brooklyn, to knock out an opponent in the boxing ring, or to work as a longshoreman, but he never told me.

I really wanted to know why he enjoyed gambling, why he eloped with Mom or what it was like to be a union organizer, but I never asked because I was afraid he would ignore me and his lack of response would convey that I was not worth his time.

We never had real conversations. We never exchanged ideas. His words to me, especially during my childhood, were directives about how to use a certain tool to pick weeds, or how to start the pull lawn mower. Perhaps if he had lived longer we would have talked.

Perhaps as I got older, I would have asked the questions I sought answers to. As I reflect now, older than my father was when he died, I feel a loss for what could have been. No one can turn back the clock, of course, but I often wonder what were the secrets he took with him to his grave.

I was the loose cannon. Now, I was the Siciliano willing to ask questions, probe and talk about what I was feeling. This was uncharacteristic and, in many ways for my brothers, very threatening, since I had usually been the invisible son and brother.

I was angry

I was angry.

I was angry and didn't know why.

By the time I was a teenager, like some of you reading this book, I had a real problem with my temper. Today professionals talk about *anger management*. We all get angry from time to time, of course, but we have to learn to control it.

When I was a teen, I didn't know the word *management*. And I had no idea why I was so angry. Many times I felt like a bubbling volcano that would erupt at any moment.

As a teenager I began to learn more about our family history, especially our New York origins.
Three individuals were raised in Brooklyn: Matteo, Alfonse and Albert.

My father Matteo arrived from Marsala out of the port of Palermo in 1913 and settled in the same area as Capone near the Navy yards in Brooklyn. They both lived in tenement flats that had no indoor plumbing, just a common toilet down the hall. By all accounts, both families were honest, good families. Both my father Matteo and Alfonse played and worked well with people of other nationalities. Even though they lived in Little Italy, my father had Jewish neighbors and Capone had German and Irish neighbors and friends.

During Al Capone's criminal career he worked easily with people of other nationalities. One of his top gunmen, Frank Guzik, was Jewish, and Capone's wife was Irish. His son, likewise, married an Irish girl.

The Little Italy of New York was teeming with people. Kids would play stickball as mothers would yell out windows for their return home,
"*E' venito la casa!*" There were the sounds of horse hooves clattering on cobblestone, and elevated trains shook windows, and rattled plates in my father's apartment. The fire escapes were a place to observe, and to sleep during hot summer nights. Capone's father was a barber, like my mother's father Guglielmo (my grandfather).

Matteo's father Vincenzo had been a Navy merchant marine and upon coming to America decided to retire. All the working children were required to pay him a monetary tribute each week. But Matteo cheated from his own father. He held back money that he used for gambling.

Both Al and Matteo liked boxing. Big Al attended boxing matches, placed bets, and got boxers to "take a dive" to win. Matteo became a boxer and won many matches in Brooklyn. But he refused to take a dive. He worked as a longshoreman as did Capone's brothers. My father and Capone's brothers knew each other as teens. This was a rough job where the Unions enforced the payment of dues and took care of strikebreakers. Matteo, my father, after getting married, became a union organizer. In those days, that meant enforcement, by whatever means necessary.

Matteo and Alfonse knew who Father Albert was. He was a parish priest in Brooklyn. They saw him at weddings and at numerous funerals. My father's excuse for not going to church was "I saw this priest coming out of one of Torrio's whore houses." It was not Father Albert but a priest from his parish.

As a teen, one of my father's hangouts was Coney Island. He would pick up girls and gambled there. At nineteen Al Capone was a bartender at the Harvard Inn at Coney Island.

As a young gang member, Capone was a member of the South Brooklyn Rippers where he was introduced to drinking, smoking, and gambling. Then he "graduated" to the Forty Thieves Juniors where he got experience fighting rival gangs and finally a member of the famous Five Points Gang run by Johnny Torrio.

Torrio was an older thug who had Capone running illegal errands for him. The Harvard Inn was a front and he let Capone handle the prostitution on the second floor when he was nineteen. Torrio was the perfect, corrupt teacher. He showed Capone how to rob, strong-arm enforcement and no doubt a murder or two. As Torrio's influence moved into Chicago, he also derived an income from Big Jim Colosimo, his uncle, a pimp who made $50,000 a month.

Capone looked up to Torrio, the godfather of his first child; Albert, Jr. At twenty-two, Capone was sent to Chicago to protect Colosimo's interests. He managed the Four Deuces speakeasy. It was Torrio who set up Dion O'Banion on Capone's request. A rival gang, led by Moran and his sidekick Weiss, shot Torrio four times. He survived, and

Big Al slept in Torrio's hospital room during his recovery. But Torrio had enough and decided to retire, turning the Chicago crime empire over to the young Capone.

What was the relationship between the Catholic Church and the Chicago mob? In 1924 Bishop Albert Mundelien (from Capone's Brooklyn neighborhood) became a Chicago cardinal receiving his red hat, at the same time Capone, O'Banion and Moran, all three Catholic gang leaders, ruled the city. A coincidence?

The priest from Brooklyn became the Bishop of Brooklyn in 1909. With the vast number of Catholics pouring into Brooklyn, he had a considerable constituency. Bishop Albert was then moved to Chicago in 1915 where he became archbishop.

Chicago never had a cardinal, but in 1924 it got the first one, Cardinal Albert Mundelein. A cardinal is an elevated title given to a bishop by the Pope, usually for having a large Catholic population and sending large amounts of money back to Peter's Pence, the Vatican's coffers. The new cardinal liked the title "Prince of the West." He had a large emerald ring framed with diamonds, a large pectoral cross of emeralds and a 20 foot scarlet train held by altar boys. He lived lavishly.

The archdiocese prospered financially during the Roaring Twenties. The cardinal had three residences, one was an elaborate 60-room mansion added to the cathedral where O'Banion sang in the choir. It was built from stone and had a four-car garage for his fleet of limousines. There was another residence further north. Mundelein had built a small city, which would become a seminary named after him, and the town Mechanics Grove was renamed Mundelein, Illinois. Did mob money help the cardinal prosper? The seminary featured a small replica of Rome with Corinthian pillars and a man-made lake. On the far side of the lake was a mansion just for the cardinal. The mansion was a copy of Mount Vernon with 600 acres of wood around a large lake, the Lake of Saint Mary.

The church still provided refuge and sanctuary for me as a teen although the "bigger picture" was looming. While I went to church often, it did not help my anger problem. The more I learned about the cardinal, my family's involvement with Capone, and my father's gambling, the angrier I got.

When I was eighteen, I was making a short film with my father's 8mm movie camera. A group of college friends and I had driven to the Indiana sand dunes. One of my lead actors and several of his friends disappeared. The sunlight was starting to fade and I was concerned that it was a wasted day. I had no idea where he went, and my anger began to fester.

It turned out they went to a bar and drank using fake IDs. The young man came back inebriated. I said, "Let's go for a walk." He knew I was angry, but he didn't know what I was planning. I leaned down as if to tie a shoelace, cupping sand in my hand. When the time seemed right and he was looking right at me, I threw the sand into his eyes. As he struggled to see, I carefully took aim and punched him in the jaw as hard as I could with a closed fist. This knocked him out. When he wakened, I leaned over, grabbed a religious medal on a chain around his neck, twisted it until I had tight control and continued to punch him in the face.

Eventually friends held me back. Days later at school, the guy had two black eyes and bruises on his face. From that point on we did not speak, and he would flinch every time I came near him. I got pleasure from his fear. I did not apologize or feel any remorse. I basically felt "he had it coming." And why did I use such a dirty tactic? Well, I wasn't sure he was not stronger than I was and the objective was to win, so disabling him, although he was already off balance from drinking, seemed totally fair to me.

In spite of such temper displays, I was a very religious kid. It seems like a contradiction, I know, but not at the time. I went to church a lot and after a few years of college, went off to seminary to study to be a priest. But none of the religious acting, the kneeling in church, the wearing of the religious garments, reduced any of my anger. I had become what I feared the most, just like my father.

To those of you who have a problem with anger, you may know the answer is simple. If you do not identify the source of the anger, what is causing the frustration, it is difficult if not impossible to solve the problem.

I was imitating my father's behavior to be sure. By the time I was a teenager, I remember telling my mother, "I never want to be anything like Dad!" Of course, sometimes we will become what we deny because of the example we witness, and Dad's explosive temper was my model.

My dad's way of solving problems was through arguments, yelling and physical blowouts. He would knock dishes to the floor, throw an ashtray at the wall, push a chair over and storm off.

When I was a child, I was told my father was angry with somebody who did not pay him a gambling debt. He beat him up so hard on a Brooklyn street that he "killed the guy," my mother told me. I don't know if he really killed the person, but that was how the story was told to me. And being a professional boxer, his fists were lethal weapons.

Between the ages of seventeen and nineteen, my anger got worse and the displays more physical. I was angry with another classmate one day (I cannot even remember why), and as we were walking I suddenly took the empty coke bottle in my hand, smashed it against a wall and held the jagged end under his neck. He was frightened, and I easily won the argument. I never got in trouble for this or other violent actions because classmates were too scared to "rat" on me to authorities. Although they were crimes in every sense of the word (assault and battery), fear insured my victim's silence.

If I got a D on a test, I would take a glass and smash it into the sink in my dorm. I lost count of how many glasses and bottles I smashed during my second year in college, but there were many. I felt safer doing it in the dorm than back at home where I would get in obvious trouble. By the time I was living at college, I was sullen, angry and depressed. I would stay up all night, walking around campus, and skip morning classes. Part of my restlessness was because I was at an age where the lack of a father and the strong air of Sicilian secrecy were beginning to take its toll.

I wanted answers. I needed answers. But most of the questions about my family would not be revealed until the walks in the mobster's cemetery with my mother.

I was nineteen when I was hospitalized for a stomach ulcer. Physically, you can only hold so many bad memories and experiences inside. My mother's quick excuse was that I was using "too much ketchup" on my hamburgers.

After several days in the hospital, an astute Italian female doctor, Marie La Goble, cornered my father during an office visit and said, "When are you going to be a father to your son? Decide between horses and him." My father screamed back, "*Cavalli*! (Horses!)" As a Sicilian man, he wasn't going to take any guff from a female doctor, and he did not like being cornered by her stern index finger. He called her several choice words like *battona* and stormed off.

After that emotional scene, I came to realize things were not going to get better between my father and I. Religion was my medication to calm my soul, but in reality I turned into a Pharisee. I became so legalistic and involved in so much ritual. It brought no peace at all except the head knowledge that I was "buying" my way to heaven. It was the only escape route I knew at the time.

I realize today I would have benefited from being able to sit down with a counselor in high school or in college and talk about my feelings, my frustrations and my family. If I was a teenager today, I certainly would. But many years were wasted with anger because I was following in the family tradition of family secrecy.

Whenever a school counselor called me in and asked, "How is your family?" I only had a one-word response, "Fine." The college psychologist summoned me in because both teachers and classmates had noticed my anger and signs of depression. The counseling session did not go far.

"How's your relationship with your father?" the psychologist asked.

"Fine," I responded.

"How was your childhood?"

"Fine," I answered.

No matter what the question, especially if it had anything to do with my family, the answer was always "Fine." I wish I had been able to tell him that I could not recall my father ever telling me he loved me in words or by putting his arm around my shoulder. I wanted to talk to somebody about his great losses as a gambling addict or the screaming arguments in my home every day, but I could not. I had learned well the social protocol and cultural mandates of full-blooded Sicilians. Every counselor and psychologist, although well meaning, was a stranger.

Dad's anger was far more than everyday consternation with every day problems. Since the days my grandfather hunted my father with a shotgun after he eloped with my underage mother, my grandfather was not high on my father's list. It was mutual. My grandfather had moved to California during the early years of my childhood. My mother saved her money for a train trip to take me to visit him. For whatever reason, my father strongly resented our trip, especially leaving for two weeks.
I was eleven and had excitedly studied the Union Pacific Railroad pamphlet. Having never been on a train. I looked forward to seeing the Rocky Mountains and visiting

southern California. A place called Disneyland had just opened. This was really my first family vacation. But my father would put a black pall over the event. I am not sure to this day why he was so angry. Most likely it was a vendetta against my grandfather. Maybe it was my mother hoarding money. I don't really know.

A taxi was coming to bring us to the Union Train Station in downtown Chicago. I thought everything was fine, but in my parent's bedroom I heard shouting and yelling. Apparently my father was taking two weeks vacation at the same time we were in California and would be at the horsetrack every day. The argument got louder.

When the taxi arrived, I was totally mortified and embarrassed when my father took our suitcases and threw them on the front lawn. They hit so hard each suitcase popped open and the clothes spilled onto the grass. Neighbors were watching, as well as the anxious cabdriver. Dad continued screaming at Mom on the front lawn as she quickly pushed all the clothes into the suitcases. She cried in the cab all the way to the train station. Then on the train she cried in private. But in the observation car she would play her accordion (she was quite accomplished) and entertained strangers, singing and playing on the train all the way to Los Angeles. The railroad porters enjoyed her music. She created a party in the observation car.

Mom feared returning home. When we got back, my father surprised her by completing a cement patio with a fiberglass awning that she always wanted. I'm sure this was his way of making up for the terrible send off. Unfortunately my mother had a habit of being critical and immediately said, "You did it all wrong! Why didn't you wait for me? It is the worst looking thing I've ever seen! (*guarda terrible!*) She told him the angle of the fiberglass was wrong, the choice of color was wrong, the cement was uneven, and of course the verbal argument ended up with him leaving in the family car, I suppose for the racetrack. And that was our welcome home. I didn't see him for three days.

The greatest manifestation of my father's anger came on a day when he was expecting to get both a raise and a bonus from his bosses at a shoe plant. Apparently he did not get the raise or the bonus and was so angry when he got home that he began throwing objects. Then he went into the small utility room off the kitchen and I heard the all too familiar creak of the rusty hinges on a small metal box. He pulled out his gun, which he usually reserved for shooting on New Year's Eve at midnight. He entered the living room looking crazed and waving the gun and saying he was going to kill the whole family and himself, ("*Vado vecidertutti!*")

My mother grabbed me by the wrist and pulled me out the front door. We began running down the block. I don't know where my brothers hid. I was seven years old and remember looking back at my father standing on our front step waving a gun. At any moment I expected to hear a shot. Neighbors watched but no one called the police. We went to the house of a girlfriend where my mother just cried and cried. I felt embarrassed and ashamed. I remember sitting alone in a room, waiting to hear a gunshot and afraid to look out a window or return home. My father smoked a few cigarettes, drank some scotch, and found a card game.

But from that day forward, I never really trusted my father. I was afraid he would shoot us in our sleep after bad gambling debts. I worried about him drinking too much and pulling out the gun almost every day.

I went to school the next day as if nothing had happened. My teachers never knew what I experienced. I sat in the classroom looking anxious and nervous while my classmates the night before had a normal dinner around a dining room table, some playing a family game together.

In fact, we never ate together as a family. I would come home from school and eat by myself on a TV snack tray

while watching television shows like *Leave it to Beaver* and
Father Knows Best. By the time my father got home hours
later, he would eat the pasta he demanded, *e fagioli*, either
alone or sitting with my mother. Then he would have two
or three drinks (whiskey) while smoking five or six
cigarettes rapidly and fall asleep watching a prizefight on
television. Eventually, Mom would tell him to come to bed
around 10:30 p.m. I went my entire high school years never
really talking to him, never sitting around a table having a
family dinner.

Of course, there were the exceptions of visiting relatives on
holidays, but my holidays were bad memories. Mom loved
to cook. That was one of the few activities, including her
music, that brought enjoyment to her life. My father would
have a formal role like carving the turkey at Thanksgiving
and she would say, "You're doing it all wrong." It really
seemed like a scary play in which people kept repeating the
same lines over and over again. Eventually Mom would
embarrass him in front of the relatives and Dad would
storm off, get into his car, and I suppose gamble
somewhere. He wouldn't return until we were all asleep.

Christmas was the same. Dad would bring home a tree,
Mom would say it was "crooked" or "scrawny," and he
would storm off. My mother was not blameless. She knew
how to push his buttons and usually did. I often wondered
if it was payback for his gambling or her exile in New York.
Both of them had so much anger and I suppose frustration,
that I rarely saw them relaxed or happy together. If they
ever held hands, hugged, or kissed, it was never in front of
the children.

As I look back, I think much of Dad's smoking and
drinking was a symptom of his stress and general
unhappiness.

Both my mother and father smoked as I grew up. There
was a perpetual cloud of cigarette smoke in the living room.

My two older brothers started smoking at an early age, too. I did not smoke but inhaled enough to do damage.

I never really saw family members drunk. My father would drink wine at the dinner table but after a day's work he preferred a strong drink, straight whiskey. In some ways it is odd that I never drank or smoked as a teenager, but not being "forbidden fruit," there was no real attraction.

Most youth assume their family's behavior is normal until they compare with others or discover things could be different. The secrecy did not help me see the larger picture.

The very Sicilian tradition of family secrets led to me being a very angry teenager in those later years of seventeen, eighteen, and nineteen. I would encourage troubled teens to talk with someone. By covering for my family and always saying that everything was "fine," I never really helped myself. Sometimes a counselor cannot solve our problems, but just having someone who understands can make a world of difference.

I don't think anyone had the power to control or change my father but himself. If I could have talked to someone about what it felt like to have my father waving a gun in front of me, or being embarrassed by having our clothes thrown out on the front lawn, it would have helped. I wanted someone to tell me it was not normal for my parents to have constant fights, verbal arguments and my father throwing and smashing things in our home. It would have helped to know just one person understood.

It was not right for me to hit my classmate or to yell or threaten so many peers. It is never an excuse to lose control because someone in your family did. It was wrong for my father to be explosive and out of control and it was wrong for me, as well.

My family became angry with me when I started talking about the family. Most of them still believe that keeping family secrets is right. There are principles more important than families that teach us bad behaviors. Mutual respect, self control, and love are far more worthy goals.

The "Little Italy" of New York City, 1920.

Don's grandfather, Guglielmo Cappitelli, produced illegal alcohol for Capone.

Don's paternal grandfather Vincenzo Smorto (far right).

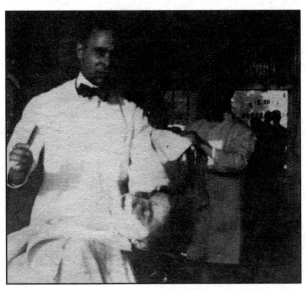

Bystanders watch Guglielmo as he shaves a prominent mobster.

Baby Rosa, Don's mother, with her parents.

Rosa at age one.

The large barbershop built by Don's grandfather.

The building where Don was born, built by his grandfather.

Don in the building foyer sixty years after it was built.

Relatives and pisano in the old neighborhood.

Rosa (far left) with sister Josephine and mother Santa.

Don's mother performs at the piano.

"Bloody Angelo" Genna, notorious hit man and relative.

Street corner where Angelo assassinated a court official.

The Terrible Genna Brother's family.

The funeral of Angelo Genna, gunned down by assassins.

Al Capone, the most famous gangster in American history.

Don visits Mt. Carmel Cemetery in 1985.

Don and his mother visit the Genna tomb in 1995.

Don looks inside the Genna crypt.

An altar beside the remains of the six slain Genna brothers.

The Cappitelli basement where family and mobsters gathered.

Rosa danced with hit men John Scalise and Alberto Anselmi.

Don's mother Rosa, as a Roaring Twenties flapper.

A crowd outside the garage where a rival gang was executed.

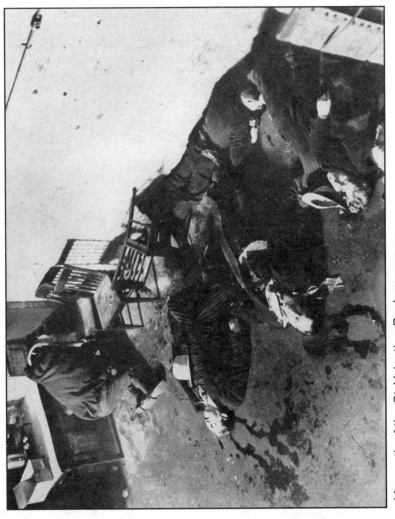

Aftermath of the St. Valentine Day's massacre.

A Thompson machine gun like the one pictured was used by Scalise and Anselmi.

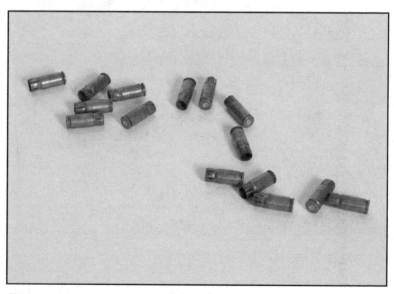

The machine gun fired 100 bullets in 6 seconds.

The flower shop where Dion O'Banion was killed by Capone's "homicide squad" Scalise and Anselmi.

The oblesik marking O'Banion's grave with bishop's tomb in the
background.

Guglielmo (center) controls the family with authority.

Capone on the cover of Time Magazine, 1925.

Big Al's personal weapon, a 45 cal.

Don and his mother visit the crypts of Capone's victims.

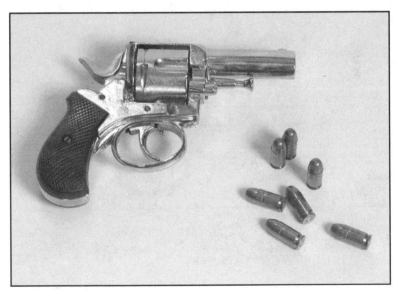

Assassin's weapon of choice, 22 cal.

Capone's Florida estate.

The first tomb of Al Capone.

Capone's simple grave today.

The Capone name is intentionally hidden by shrubs.

*Rosa' father at the height of his wealth and power, looking like Brando in **The Godfather**.*

Scalise, Anselmi, and Angelo Genna attended parties in Rosa's home.

Rosa's protective cousins suspected a secret romance.

Matteo's love of horses began early.

Don's father Matteo was a successful Brooklyn prize fighter.

Rosa married against her will at age 16.

Don's father Matteo at the time of his marriage at age 21.

Matteo's "bodyguard" Sammy (left) guarded the couple.

Guglielmo holding the shotgun he hunted Matteo with.

Rosa living in poverty in Brooklyn with her first child.

Grandfather Smorto's home funeral.

Don's brothers Anthony and Joseph with toy guns.

Matteo's in-laws strike an uncomfortable pose.

Relatives in the old neighborhood.

Guglielmo's new car, a Chandler.

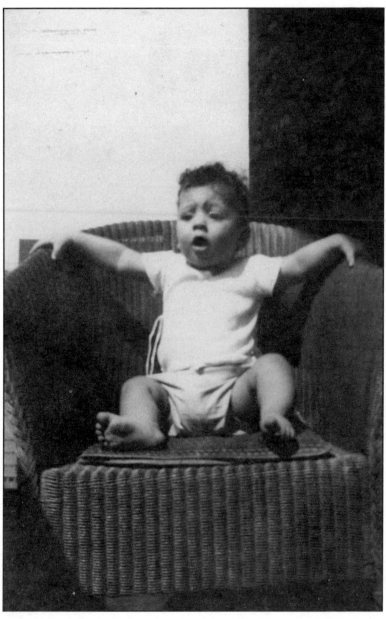

Don as a baby.

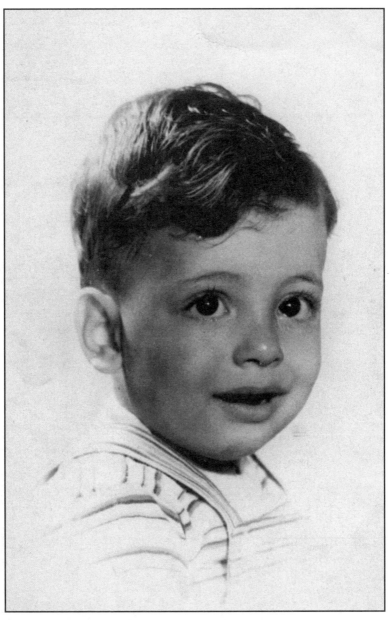

Don, age one.

Rosa with her three sons, holding "Donnie", the youngest.

Don (L) looked up to his older brother, Anthony.

Don's second home, a place of discord.

Don with his mother.

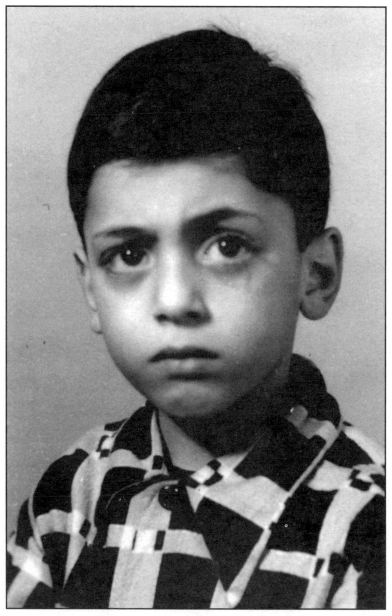

"Donnie", an unhappy child witnesses marital strife.

The three brother (L to R) Joseph, Anthony, and "Donnie".

Don's real godfather, Giovanni.

Don's father Matteo, a compulsive gambler.

Don watches his father (center) playing poker.

Many of Matteo's card games had high stakes.

A family bartender from age eight, Don serves Anthony.

Don's role models, brothers, Joseph and Anthony.

Rosa dressed for a nightclub.

Sam Giancana's Villa Venice Club.

Chicago boss, Sam "Momo" Giancana.

Rosa at Sam's tomb, a mafia capo.

Photos on Italian headstones with palm crosses.

Don, an angry and frustrated teenager.

Don's ordination as a Roman Catholic cleric.

*Rosa as nightclub entertainer **Rose Carmen**.*

Don's mother performing at a Chicago nightclub.

Hoffa confronts Robert Kennedy.

Joe Valachi testifies about the mob.

Sinatra with crime figures.

Seconds before President Kennedy is fatally shot in Dallas.

Don and Regina get engaged.

Don's large Italian wedding.

Don with brothers, Joseph (L), Anthony (R).

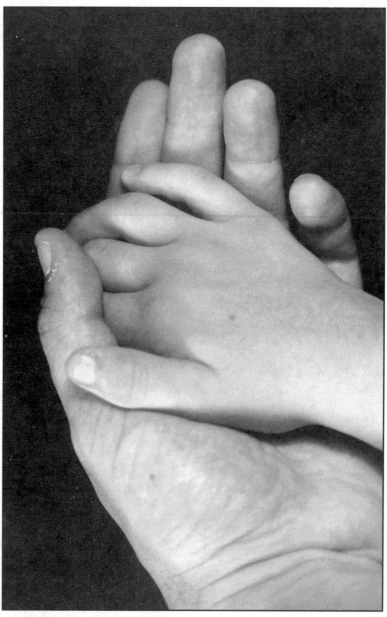

Don holds his son Luke's hand.

One of Don's favorite photos of his wife, Regina.

Luke with his grandmother Rosa.

Anthony calls himself "The Godfather".

Anthony's crimes makes headlines.

Regina's family with Rosa (center) in 1996.

Don with Russian warden and journalist, 1992.

A million dollar tomb replicates a cathedral (Mt. Carmel Cemetery).

Note bullet holes in stained glass window.

Don with President Ronald Reagan.

Rosa's last visit to Mt. Carmel Cemetery at age eighty-two.

Don's awards as video / film director.

Don is the host of the radio show Parenting Today's Youth.

7

I was apprehensive

I was apprehensive.

I was apprehensive about the people who came into our home, played cards in a back room and had jobs that did not match their expensive cars, jewelry and clothes. They were part of something sinister, but no one talked about their "work."

You can learn a lot by being quiet. I was a quiet child. Some relatives thought I was "slow" but did not realize that a quiet child can be listening intently.

I looked, observed, listened, and I learned.

My mother would take me for visits to *il cimitero* (the cemetery). Like my grandfather, she called this "visiting the dead." "*Visitare i morti,*" my grandfather called it. It really was a good form of education and oral history. As we would stop at the headstones and what I thought of as the "little houses" (mausoleums), she would recount stories. It did not seem like a morbid activity. To a child, it was a park with a lot of stone.

The cemetery we visited most frequently was Mount Carmel in Hillside, west of Chicago. In this cemetery was buried, in *avello* (tombs) perched high on a hill, the *princes* of the church, that is, *il cardinale* (the cardinals) of Chicago. The best real estate was the property facing the cardinals' tombs. Assuming their bones were holy, this would somehow extend that saintliness to the departed close by.

But these hallowed grounds were also the final resting place of the Chicago mob. Those who assassinated each other were often buried within several feet of each other. Between 1924 and 1930 more people buried there died from bullets than heart disease and cancer.

I witnessed something strange when I was younger. There was a woman dressed in black, sometimes wearing a veil that my mother would meet in the cemetery. She never explained who the lady was. They would have animated conversations in Italian while sitting on a concrete bench. Who was this mysterious woman? "*La signora in nero,*" (the lady in black) my mother called her. Why did they only meet in the cemetery?

One day, I saw the woman fastening something to one of the crypts. It was an Italian Catholic tradition to take a palm from Palm Sunday services and fashion it into a cross and attach it to the handle of the mausoleum door. This would help the souls of the departed get out of purgatory faster, according to belief. The crypt had a family name inscribed in stone—GENNA.

As a boy, I would peer in the door's window and count six crypts with the names of six Genna brothers. Their names were Angelo, Michael, Peter, Samuel, James and Anthony. The strange fact of the dates of their deaths was the proximities. Angelo, Mike and Pete died the same year, each a month apart in April, May and June of 1925.

Their photos appeared in our family album, as they did in history books. These were not only family friends but also *consanguineo* (blood relatives). When my mother was in her late seventies, she began unraveling many of the mysteries for me. She was not only a witness to many gangland events, but our family was involved more than I ever guessed or suspected.

The Gennas all came from the same town in Sicily as my grandparents and my father: Marsala. In Chicago they were called *The Terrible Gennas*. They started with Black Hand activities called *Mano Nero*. They would literally extort from their fellow Sicilians in the Little Italy section of Chicago. They demanded money on the "Sunday collection" to bring other relatives to America from Sicily. One did not have a choice. If you refused to give the Gennas money, you might have an accident or your house would catch on fire. Sometimes it was called "protection money" or insurance. My grandfather would say to his wife, *"Prima paghi meglio é."* (The sooner you pay, the better.)

In reality, they were recruiting "soldiers," not military, of course. These were ruthless killers who were fleeing from the police in Sicily and were brought to America to become part of the Genna's growing crime operation. The Genna brothers had brought over from Sicily two of the most ruthless and vicious murderers in American history. The tall, thin John Scalise and the portly, short Alberto Anselmi were both wanted for murder in Marsala. My mother saw both of them frequently. They were guests in our home. She would serve them Italian pastries and serenade them singing and playing the accordion.

The Genna brothers were superstitious young men. Each kept a crucifix in his pocket, touching his gun. Rarely did they use holsters. The gun of choice was usually small, a .22 caliber. Only when they needed to do greater damage would they use a machine gun, nicknamed the "tommy gun," which in the early twenties was not illegal to own. They would also finish off enemies with a shotgun at close range to the face as final disrespect. But the .22 was an intimate weapon. You had to get close to your victim. Angelo's nickname was *Bloody Angelo*, and he earned it.

Angelo was angry at a court official, and one day on the corner of State and Madison in downtown Chicago, an extremely busy corner at the lunch hour, he walked up to the official, shot him behind his left ear and after his body collapsed to the ground, shot him several more times in the chest, *a sangue freddo* (in cold blood). Angelo had a devilish stare that could look right through you. If ever there was a cold-blooded killer, it was Angelo. He slowly walked away from the lifeless body with the gun in hand, and the barrel still smoking. There were upwards of a thousand people at that intersection and yet there were no witnesses. Fellow Sicilians would say of him, *"Non cé nicente che possa spaventario.* (Nothing can scare him.)"

Prohibition made the manufacture or selling of alcohol illegal. The law derived from a moral movement to eradicate drunkenness in America, but actually resulted in the Mafia gaining power and much wealth.

The Gennas were good businessmen. They realized the basic laws of supply and demand and began producing alcohol that they and Al Capone would sell. Capone probably never really trusted them, but the business arrangement was mutually beneficial. The Gennas would produce crude alcohol for 40 cents a gallon and sell it for $40 a gallon.

My mother remembered the Genna brothers well. *"Gentilvomini,"* (gentlemen) my grandmother, Santa, would say of them. She was frequently in their homes for parties.

She remembered Tony, nicknamed *The Gentleman*, "pinning $50 and $100 bills to an American flag hung on his wall at a birthday party." Mom continued, "It was in a beautiful wood paneled apartment with high ceilings on the Gold Coast." (Lake Shore Drive north of the city) The Genna brothers were cousins of my grandfather.

I mostly remember my grandfather as an older, temperamental man who only spoke Italian and had been a barber. Gradually I learned more. My grandfather came from Sicily in 1913 at age 25 with no possessions, no money, and although he had barber skills, because he could not write and read in English, could not take the barber test. He worked for the railroad for two years and eventually got his barber's license.

I could never figure out how a young man without money or education did so well for himself. Within ten years, my grandfather had built a barbershop on Harrison and hired three employees. Then he built a large apartment building with four flats. He was the first in his neighborhood to have *uno macchina nuovo* (a brand new car), a Chandler, the first to have a grand piano, a Victrola, and a large wood Cathedral radio. His wife and children were dressed well, and my grandfather had diamond rings.

It was the basement of my grandfather's apartment building that was the scene of many parties. Relatives would come on Sunday afternoons for a lavish feast. His acquired wealth funded his generosity.

"A salute" is a toast to the head of the household, sipping a dark, red, Chianti wine. My mother helped my grandmother in the kitchen. Immigrant Italian women had a romance with food. After the minestrone soup came a large bowl of pasta, the egg noodles made fresh that morning, rolled out onto a floured sheet on one of the beds, a sight I saw hundreds of times. As a child I would take the raw dough and eat it, when no one was looking.

With the shortage of meat in the impoverished towns and cities of Sicily, pizza became a staple. It consisted of few ingredients, unlike the "Supreme" American pizza with six or seven ingredients. It was thin dough with hand-crushed tomatoes, pieces of buffalo mozzarella, extra virgin olive oil and basil leaves. Originally meant as a quick outdoor sandwich for the returning fishermen, it was folded, and hand eaten, point first.

The *Napoletana* (those from Naples) insisted they invented pizza, as did the Sicilians. Perhaps both did because of the fishing industry.

My mother and her mother, Santa, used their hands as they cooked. Never using tomatoes from a can, mom would crush tomatoes in her hand. She rolled the pasta by hand, too. The pesto sauce was ground by hand. Olive oil, pine nuts, grated cheese and pecorino were not measured by graded cups. It was a pinch of this and a handful of that.

How did my grandfather fund so many parties? His money did not come only from the barbershop, however, but from producing illegal alcohol for the Genna brothers and ultimately for Capone. He had a large *cooker* behind the barbershop and in the basement of his home and would visit the distillery on Taylor to assist with larger quantities. By all accounts, my grandfather and his Sicilian cohorts were able to produce 700 gallons of illegal alcohol a week, with Angelo their boss.

My mother remembered "Bloody" Angelo well. He was always dressed in beautiful suits, a black overcoat with a velvet collar, brocade vests, spats over shoes, and a broad brimmed Fedora hat, which he took off out of courtesy when he entered our house. Mom would notice my grandfather's hands slightly trembling when he poured the Chianti wine into Angelo's *bicchiereda vino* (wine glass). Bloody Angelo would always give a toast to the head of the household, my grandfather, "*Salutati. Dio vi benedica!* (May God bless you!)" He was always wearing two; maybe three guns, and having killed hundreds of men, may have come straight from a "job" before visiting my grandfather's building. His large black sedan was parked in front with bodyguards at the front and back entrances.

I was born in that building and lived on the top floor during my early childhood. When I played in the basement, the parties for the Capone and Genna gangsters were long gone but not gone from my mother's memories. "*E' peccato* (It's a pity)," she would murmur, sad that the festivities were over.

My mother recounted Angelo's wedding, which she attended with my grandparents. "He was living with Gladys Bagwell, the daughter of a Baptist minister," Mom related as old gossip, "but courting a Mafia princess." And upon marriage, since he and his brothers were making well over two millions dollars a year (before taxes), Angelo hosted one of the largest weddings in the history of Chicago. He married not his mistress but the daughter of one of Al Capone's lawyers, Henry Spignola. It was a society wedding, of sorts, the melding of several crime families. The reception was held in a large armory. The wedding cake was so tall, my mother Rosa remembered, "A large Fire Department ladder was used to cut the top piece of the cake." These mobsters were generous and wanted to show off their affluence. Thousands attended. My mother remembered the excitement of the event.

A month later, however, fearing that the Gennas were getting too powerful, Al Capone sent several of his men to eliminate Bloody Angelo. With pockets stuffed with cash, he was on route to purchase their newlywed home.

It was May 1925 and Angelo was driving in an open roadster when he approached the intersection of Ogden and Hudson. Two cars pulled along side. As he sped up, Angelo hit a tree that pinned him between the wheel and the seat. He watched as six men stood up in the cars alongside him firing machine guns and finishing him off with four shotguns. That was a Sicilian "hit" tradition of a shotgun blast to the face so that the departed gangster could not have an open casket for his family.

My grandparents were sad. Grandma Santa said *"Mori perdonando ai suoi nemici* (He died forgiving his enemies)," a nice tribute but hardly true. He died cursing his enemies. Angelo looked intently at his killers, *si odianoa vicenda* (hating each other).

The largest wedding in Chicago was soon followed by the largest funeral. My mother attended that event, also. There were thirty-two cars of flowers and a procession down the main streets of Taylor and Maxwell in Little Italy. The entire community turned out. Mom said, "It was like a parade with a band and a long procession." The surviving five brothers carried a floral tribute. One enormous floral piece sent condolences from "Big Al" written on a satin sash.

My grandfather wore a black armband and walked with his *Union brothers* in the procession. Those in the crowd whispered, *"Sparare a morte.* (He was gunned down.)"

My mother told me, "I remember the funeral procession for Angelo Genna like it was yesterday. It was sad and no one knew why he was killed...except for our family. There were more cars than you could count, over 30 just with flowers. And they had his car towed on a truck with black draping on it. You could see the holes the bullets made."

Soon after killing Bloody Angelo, the killers went to the office of his father-in-law, Henry Spignola. He was shot and killed based on the "theory" that he would seek retaliation for his son-in-law's killing. His mausoleum is only several feet from the Genna mausoleum.

Public officials sent flowers and telegrams and the courageous attended. Mobsters like Al Capone and Bloody Angelo only survived through *the fix.* They were able to carry off their criminal activities because they paid bribes to public officials. Angelo had on his payroll five police captains, 400 police officers and 20 lawyers from the state attorney's office.

Al Capone paid bribes to judges, police officers, mayors, congressmen and governors, too. These gangsters could never have gotten so wealthy or so powerful or evaded arrest for violent crimes if there was not official corruption. In fact, corrupt police and elected officials (*corrompere i funzionari*) were the ones who benefited monetarily by looking the other way.

My grandmother Santa said to Mom after Angelo's funeral, "*Nonostante i soi difetti, e' un buon vomo.* (In spite of his faults, he was a good man.)" My mother agreed.

Some of the men who came into my grandfather's basement were Ralph Capone (Al's brother), Tony Lombardo, and Smoots Amatuna. Also, at his barbershop, only he would shave Big Al, the Genna brothers and other notorious gang members. Capone's car was a black armored sedan and when it was parked outside my grandfather's barbershop, a crowd would gather, looking in the window. With my grandfather holding a straight razor to Capone's neck, his bodyguards paid extra attention. Mostly, my grandfather went to Capone's hotels. It was safer for *Scarface*.

Sicilian women were not supposed to be involved in the *business* of their husbands. They cooked and entertained. My mother was a singer and a piano player and would often perform for many of these men. They enjoyed the Italian songs from the old country that she would sing in the native language with her distinct Sicilian accent. If someone talked during a song, others would say "*Zitto!* (Quiet!) *Ascolta la canzone.* (Listen to the song.)" Her mother, my grandmother Santa, would be busy cooking and serving the food, while her father, Guglielmo, beamed with pride.

Because she spoke fluent Italian, mother heard the conversations about the Genna's anger with other ethnic gangs. There was *Il nemico* (the enemy), Dion O'Banion, the powerful Irish gang leader who controlled the north side and Bugs Moran, the German gang leader who controlled part of the west side. Not recalling Capone killed the Genna brothers, Mom looked up to Al Capone as a hero.

Capone moved around to several locations having hideouts in Wisconsin, Elgin, Illinois, Kansas City and St. Louis and had dinners at the top of the Allerton Hotel on Michigan Avenue, but his headquarters were at the Hawthorne Hotel in Cicero. Cicero was a town that he literally took captive.

Al Capone had a thousand employees and almost all were gunmen. He could literally sway an election. At the polling place, one of Capone's men would stand next to a voter, holding a gun if need be or just keeping his hand in his pocket. The "correct" votes would go into the ballot box. The "incorrect" votes would be torn up and the person would be given a second chance to make it right.

Word got out that Capone was trying to put in his own guy as the mayor of Cicero and the Chicago police sent several carloads of armed police to chase the enforcers out. The town was controlled by Capone's brother, Frank, and a gun battle ensued just like something out of the movies. Frank was hit several times and died. The death of Big Al's brother enraged him, but on a positive note, Capone won the election. Unfortunately, the mayor, Ed Konvalinka, thought he really had power when in reality he was simply a puppet for the Capone organization. One day, after a ruling at city hall that Capone did not like there was a confrontation on the front steps of city hall. Capone knocked the mayor to the ground and repeatedly kicked him while the Cicero police looked the other way. From that point on, the mayor got the message.

One day in 1994 when Mom was older, we were at a Chicago exhibit that had a robotic mannequin of Al Capone and his gang at a tourist exhibit on the corner of State and Ohio in Chicago. She was quiet during the presentation. Then my wife and I took her to the souvenir shop where there were T-shirts with Al Capone's silk-screened face. We will never forget how upset she got.

"This is not funny!" she exclaimed. *"Mancansa di rispetto,"* (disrespect) she said forcefully. "He did a lot of good for his people and this is just making fun of him!"

That's when I began to suspect that he was not just a legendary crime figure from the movies for her. There were some obvious relationships as she was still defending him forty years after his death.

One day at the Hillside cemetery, we stopped at the mausoleum of Michael Merlo. He was the President of the Unione Sicilione. This was the prestigious organization of Sicilians that worked together for better wages, opposed unjust taxes and oppression by the Irish and German politicians, and, of course, was a front for Mafia crime including the bootlegged whiskey of the prohibition era. Even though he had died in 1924, she would still gesture by making the sign of the cross and then kissing her fingertips, a gesture that she was still praying for his immortal soul to be released from purgatory. She told me "it was really the union of death." (*i'unione di morte*) A cousin of my grandfather, Angelo Genna, was the successor to Mike Merlo, but eight union presidents in a row were killed, including Sam Smoots, followed by Tony Lombardo, Pasqualino Lolerdo, Joe Juinta, and Joe Aiello. Who killed them? Of course they were unsolved crimes in the 1920s and early 1930s, but we have a good guess it was Al Capone's assassins. My grandfather was a union member but had no desire to seek the presidency of the union. He knew too much.

In movies like *The Untouchables*, Robert DeNiro, an actor in his late forties, played Al Capone. In real life Capone was twenty-six years old at the height of his power. It was a myth that he was an immigrant. He was actually born in New York, not in Italy, and his parents came from Naples. This may not seem important, but since he was Neopolitan and the true Mafia came from Sicily, he was always envious that he could never be president of the Sicilian Union. Like so many of the mobsters, Al started as a juvenile gang member. He was a member of the James Street Gang, run by Johnny Torrio who introduced him to serious crimes. He then graduated into the Five Points Gang with fellow members like Lucky Luciano. The juvenile gang was a great training place for these future Mafiosi. Capone started his criminal career in gambling and prostitution, but after being sought by the police for murder, he moved to Chicago in 1919. The New York gang members kept close ties with Capone and eventually turned over an organization with a thousand members and a payroll of $300,000 per week.

Capone got more attention than the mayor and the President of the United States. When he entered a Chicago baseball park, he got a standing ovation. He freely gave interviews to the press and reporters sought him out.

Al was famous but still had to battle with rivals and enemies. Dion O'Banion never had a personal bodyguard because he felt invincible. O'Banion kept Capone and the Genna brothers out of the north side with their alcohol. They solved their problem with several rounds.

After the execution of Bloody Angelo, Scalise and Anselmi gave their total allegiance to Capone. A few weeks later they took Mike "The Devil" Genna for a ride, which was actually a set-up to bring him to the police. When the police (who were paid off) began firing, Scalise and Anselmi ran away down an alley as Mike was shot in the leg.

My family knew the story that Chicagoans did not hear. Mike kicked one of the police officers in the groin as he was spouting an expletive at him. The cops paid the ambulance driver to take the "long way." His leg injury was not life threatening except the ten-minute ride to the hospital turned into two hours. Mike bled to death in the ambulance.

A month later, Peter Genna was gunned down, and brothers Sam, Jim and Tony fled to Sicily. Capone was able to reach Sam and Jim, but Tony was imprisoned in Sicily for stealing the jewels from a statue of the Madonna in a church. That news really bothered Mom. Killing was acceptable for "business" but not stealing from the Virgin Mary (*Rubare dal Mary Vergine*).

When Tony Genna thought it was safe after several years, he came back to America. Again, my family knew his real demise. The official story was that he was having routine surgery and died during the operation. The true story was that Capone's successors paid the doctor to nick an artery during the surgery. True, "he died during the surgery but with help," my mother said, "the sister told me and she would know." The six brothers were in coffins in their mausoleum and the mysterious woman that my mother met with was their sister, of course. Now both in their early eighties, having communicated all these years, she still insisted to my mother that she did not understand why anyone would want to kill her brothers. Denial is a strong force, especially with Sicilian women.

My mother knew they were planning something special in her basement when the large black sedans were parked in both the street front and back alleys in 1929. These were bodyguards of mob figures, cousins and *paisanos*. After the attempted assassination of Capone, a reporter asked if he had any idea who had tried to kill him. Capone responded by saying, "Watch the morgue." Clearly he was going to take justice into his own hands. The basement meetings increased, they talked of what to do with Bugs Moran and the other rival gang leaders.

It was my mother's birthday and there was a party for her in the large basement. There was abundant wine, food and music. That night she was dancing alternately with Scalise and Anselmi. She never suspected they were wearing three guns, nor what they had planned for the following week. It is still an unsolved crime.

Frank "Bugs" Moran received a phone call that friends were bringing a hijacked truck with Canadian liquor to his garage at 2122 N. Clark Street. Moran told the caller to bring the truck the next morning. February 14, 1929, at 10:30 a.m. Walking down the street near the garage were Anselmi and Scalise dressed in civilian clothes and holding packages wrapped in newspaper. A fake police car arrived in front of the garage. One driver, Sam, was dressed in a police uniform and two of Capone's men, including McGurn, dressed as police officers entered the garage. A second police car stood as backup. Among the men in the garage were the owner of Hyer's Garage, Adam Hyer, and gangster brothers Frank and Pete Gusenberg, seven men in all. The "police officers" told them it was a raid. There were seven trucks parked in the garage filled with rum that was about to be shipped to Detroit. That is what Moran's men thought the raid was about. Moran and two of his men came around the corner in their car and saw the *police* entering the building. They decided to keep on driving, which saved Moran's life.

Scalise and Anselmi waited in the hallway, removed the newspaper and held the contents of their packages. The seven Moran associates, his key men, and the garage owner were actually calm when told to "line up against the wall." It was a procedure they had been through before. They knew they had a *fix* at the police station and would soon be back on the streets. So by all accounts they were relaxed, cooperative, smiling. In fact, Frank looked over to his brother, Pete, and winked, my mother heard in a conversation that evening.

The deadly duo remained patient as the police impersonators played their charade. As the Moran gang prepared to be frisked, Scalise and Anselmi checked their weapon of choice for this job; the Thompson Submachine Gun model 1921. The gun was nine pounds with an additional eight pound 100 round drum of Colt .45 caliber cartridges.

"Okay, boys!" one of the policemen shouted.

With quick, sure steps, the two entered the garage and took position a mere 15 feet in back of the seven men lined up against the brick wall. The experienced team aimed their 10 inch barrels low, knowing the muzzles would climb naturally from the explosive pressure and gas behind each projectile, sending lead into their victim's backs and heads. The assassins opened fire with one long deafening roar. The muzzles spewed flames as a hail of copper jacketed bullets ripped into flesh. In six seconds, 200 bullets were fired, a shower of shiny brass casings hitting the greasy concrete floor. Outside, people walking through the light snowfall were jarred by the blast of noise. They stood motionless. All sound stopped, as an echo trailed off. Seeing the police cars and uniformed drivers, they assumed a shoot-out, not a hit.

The machine guns still smoked as Anselmi pronounced proudly, "*Questo é un levoro benfatto.* (This is a job well done.)" These were the "distinguished gentlemen" my mother had danced with only days before.

Surprisingly, at least three were still alive. That is when the "police" pulled out the sawed off shotguns held under their coat by a hook and finished off Moran's gang members. The sight of the police cars (my family knew there were three, not one, as seen in films and written accounts) and sounds of gunfire attracted a crowd outside, but the *assassino* had an escape plan. Scalise and Anselmi in civilian clothes put their hands in the air while the men dressed as police officers led them out at gunpoint to the waiting police van, appearing to arrest them. "*Cammina velocre.* (Walk fast.)" said McGurn, who spoke Italian.

The first pedestrian who dared to enter the garage saw a haze of smoke still lingering in the air and exclaimed, "*Bagno di sangue!* (Blood bath!)"

Within minutes Sam had brought the black Cadillac he drove to a yard where friends cut it in pieces with an acetylene torch. Tony Capezio, a family friend, had the assignment of torching one of the St. Valentine's Day getaway cars. His acetylene torch blew up a reserve gas tank that he was unaware of. He had serious burns and went to an emergency room for treatment. By the time the police arrived, he had disappeared. The engine block was dynamited and ended up in a town called Maywood Park. Pieces of the car were spread to junkyards around Chicago. This was known by my family but not by the police, just as my grandfather knew where the uniforms were burned.

Scalise, Anselmi and several drivers attended a St. Valentine's Day party in my grandfather's basement that evening. Cheery and calm, they were celebrating a victorious workday. Mom's uncle, Pasqualino, gave advise to the *sicario* (hit men) acting as *consigliere* (counselor).

That week Capone was in Florida at his Palm Island estate, a beautiful cream-colored, two-story, Italian villa with large arched windows and boathouse for one of his favorite activities, fishing. When reporters arrived later that day, he claimed no knowledge. Bugs Moran, on the other hand, said, "Only Capone kills like that." Moran wasn't stupid. He left the state and lived out the rest of his life in exile.

One Italian photographer from the Chicago American newspaper was always good to Capone and photographed him from his good side, not showing his scar. His name was Tony Berardi.

An unsolved crime according to Chicago authorities, but my family knew exactly who did it. Also, my grandfather knew Capone's favorite press photographer (Berardi), as he came into his barbershop for haircuts. He was given a tip so he would have exclusive photos before others arrived. In private, he told my grandfather he actually dragged several of the bodies closer together to get a better "group shot." The photograph appeared on the cover of many newspapers, but no one, other than the photographer, my grandparents, and of course Mom, knew the bodies had been repositioned.

My grandfather Guglielmo told his daughter Rosa after the St. Valentine's Day Massacre, "They let Tony get in first to get the good pictures." My mother told me years later that "Berardi had to drag a few bodies (*ha trascinato i corpi*). They were too spread out."

She added, "They didn't have one car painted to look like a police car, they had three." This would account for why several cars were identified as the car of the St. Valentine's Day massacre. Historical accounts only name one auto. (Actually a van.)

The Sicilian Union President was now Joe Juinta. Joe had conspired with Scalise and Anselmi to overthrow Capone. At this stage it was just talk, but it had gotten back to Capone.

If you ever saw the film **The Untouchables,** you may remember a scene in which Capone takes out a baseball bat. In the movie he clubs one person, but it was actually three. It was an Indian club called a *bastoncione,* which is shorter and heavier. After smashing Juinta over the head at the table, McGurn and other bodyguards held down Scalise and Anselmi. They were personally beaten to death by Capone and given no time to pray, unlike a 1960's film with actor Rod Steiger.

People like Capone and the Gennas had no respect for faith or spirituality. In fact, when one man started praying in front of Bloody Angelo, Angelo first shot off his hands before killing him.

The bodies of Juinta, Scalise and Anselmi were thrown on the roadside so they could be found. Capone had a secret burial place on a northern Indiana farm when he wanted people to disappear, but when he wanted to warn other members of the seriousness of talking about betrayal, he made sure the bodies were found.

After the President of the Sicilian Union, Joe Guinta, was beaten by a club at his own testimonial dinner by Capone,

Joe Aiello became the new President of the Union. Aiello's Sicilians produced illegal alcohol for Capone but wasn't sharing enough of the profits with Big Al. Capone publicly humiliated him, made him get on his knees and plea for mercy. But Aiello did not learn his lesson. He put a contract out on Capone and said he would pay $50,000 to any hit man who could prove he had killed Big Al. That brought in Torcho from New York, Russo from Cleveland, Spicuzza from St. Louis, and Volante from New Orleans. Like a group of bounty hunters from the Old West, they were confident they could kill Al Capone.

Capone took care of each of the hired gunmen one at a time. Some say McGurn was the triggerman. Each dead "hit man" had a bright shiny nickel in his hand, symbolic of how much of the $50,000 he received. (Someone still leaves shiny nickles at Capone's headstone.) Aiello hid in a friend's apartment. He had train tickets to the Mexican border. On October 23, 1930, he stepped into a taxicab. As he did, three machine guns fired from a second floor window wounding Aiello but he got away. As he ran down an alley, he pulled out his automatic, but at the end of the alley from another window, two machine guns riddled him with 60 bullets. Some of his friends were also killed the same day. A wreath was sent to each funeral. The largest to Joe Aiello's with an inscription on the ribbon "from Big Al."

Yet, another funeral for my grandparents and mother and more grave plots and mausoleums for her to visit. Scalise and Anselmi's bodies were shipped back to Sicily for burial, however. Beyond the headlines, these victims were frequent houseguests and men who had danced with my mother. The young driver of the St. Valentine's Day Massacre, Momo, was Sam Giancana, who later would become Tony Accardo's driver and a crime boss in the tradition of Capone in the 1950s and 60s and a friend (Amico) of my parents.

Because of the abrupt way my mother and father were married, Mom always talked about the death of her mother and how soon afterwards my grandfather abruptly left Chicago, buying a farm in California.

I could never figure out why my grandfather suddenly left the city, although it was right after Capone died. Did he lose his protection? I may never know the full story. The innocent, old man I remember was not only involved in crime but knew much, which can sometimes be a dangerous thing.

I was next in line

I was next in line.

I was next in line, but didn't know where I was headed. If I was to follow in my family's footsteps, where would they take me? Just how powerful were my "uncles"? What did they really do outside of their homes?

I watched an endless stream of politicians come to my godfather's home, aldermen, congressmen, high ranking police as well as priests who joined the backroom card games with my many "uncles." Most were involved in the continuous stream of phone calls and fixed horse-racing.

Capone, O'Banion, Moran and the Terrible Genna's only became powerful because they had politicians, judges and police captains in their pockets, through bribery.

What happened when officials decided to become honest reformers? One strong mayor of Chicago, William Dever, actually forced Capone to move to Cicero, a suburb immediately south of the city. When Capone tried to put his own mayor in the town of Cicero, Dever sent 79 police officers wearing plain clothes, in unmarked cars all holding shotguns to enforce honesty. Capone's own brother, Frank, was killed during a shootout with Dever's men. Capone was unforgiving.

When a politician blocked the mob in a big way, bosses like Capone resorted to what was called the "Italian Solution (*soluzione italiana*)." That usually meant someone had to be eliminated, in plain language *die*. At the height of Capone's power, although he was under federal investigation, a new mayor was elected in 1931, Mayor Anton Cermak. The mayor made it his platform to "drive the mob out." Cermak said in his first address, "In Chicago, there will be no hoodlums left!" Never had a public official, no less "His Honor" himself, the Mayor of the City of Chicago, ever defied Capone so openly. As a result, Cermak traveled with bodyguards and wore a bulletproof vest, at least when he was in Chicago. My grandfather thought his days were limited.

On February 15, 1933, Cermak joined President-elect Roosevelt. They were in an open car in Miami when according to history, Guiseppi Zangera, a lone assassin attempted to kill the President-elect but instead "shot the mayor by mistake," according to the press.

Cermak lived several days and said bluntly, "The Capone mob is responsible." The government's rush to judgment was a "lone assassin" explanation. For political reasons, according to my family, the government said Zangera wanted to kill the future President and suffered from tremendous stomach pains. He was promptly executed within the year. But an autopsy showed no stomach problems or illness of any kind. According to my mother, "They got Cermak. Then they named a street after him."

Zangera was a compulsive gambler at the racetrack and owed considerable money to the mob. He was truly present but must have been a remarkably bad marksman since every shot missed Roosevelt at close range. My uncle, Filippo, said there was a Capone hit man standing near Zangera. Oddly, Zangera had a .32 gun, but Cermak was hit by a .45. Was it a Capone hit? He was in prison at the time, but that did not stop him from controlling mob revenge, through his trusted underboss Frank Nitti. Was this family "business" capable of changing government? My father was not cynical but realistic about who government officials "were in bed with," in his words.

I attended the Melrose Park Feast every summer in the 1950s in an Italian town outside Chicago. It was a religious festival (celebrating Our Lady of Mt. Carmel) to raise money for the church but was really a carnival. The church used the large gravel parking lot of the Maywood Racetrack for the rides, booths and a main stage. Only top Italian performers *I cantanti Italiani famosi* (famous Italian singers) sang, people like Connie Francis, Al Martino, and Dick Contino.

Who was the greatest Italian performer at the time? Of course, the chairman of the board, Frank Sinatra. Over the years, Sinatra claimed that he did not have any friendships or associations with members of the mob. This was difficult to believe.

Key mob figures in New York, Miami, Chicago and Las Vegas were frequently in his dressing room for photos and private meetings when he performed. Family members talked of seeing Sinatra at parties and receptions attended by key mob figures at the Villa Venice in Chicago and the Fountainbleau in Miami.

In the motion picture *The Godfather*, there is more than a veiled reference to a young singer who seeks a part in a war movie. Sinatra himself had a resurgence of his career by appearing in the film *From Here to Eternity*.

By the 1950s the mob was heavily involved in most unions. With control of the Teamsters Union, the mob would say the word and stop trucking across America. This enabled them to halt the movement of equipment in the motion picture industry. Also, all the projectionists across America were unionized and mob-controlled. Say the word, and equipment would malfunction, so the motion picture industry had crime family control.

While my parents did not go to restaurants often, they did go to clubs frequently. These were nightclubs in New York City where my mother enjoyed dressing in a gown and mink stole she borrowed because of their poverty. My father would always have a shiny silver suit with matching tie. I never went with them but heard about it from my mother the next morning. One of their favorite Chicago clubs was the Villa Venice. In the early 1960s, the Rat Pack, which included Sinatra, Dean Martin and Sammy Davis, Jr., played at the Villa Venice in Wheeling. In fact, they had an exclusive engagement for six performances.

Later when the FBI questioned members of the Rat Pack and asked how much they were paid, the answer was, "Gratis." These high salaried performers played at the Villa Venice for free. Why?

Did Sinatra have mob connections? My family believed so. When his career began in 1946, he was seen at a hotel in Havana, Cuba, with famous mobster Lucky Luciano of the New York family. Luciano had been a fellow young gang member with Al Capone. Sinatra was also part owner of a Las Vegas casino with Myer Lansky, a well-known Jewish mobster, and later, Sinatra had an exclusive engagement to play at a Las Vegas casino, the Sands Hotel, also mob controlled.

Other members of the Rat Pack included Joey Bishop, a comedian and writer, and actor Peter Lawford. Peter Lawford had married the sister of a Massachusetts senator named John Kennedy. John Kennedy's father, Joseph P. Kennedy, had worked with Capone and other members of the mob supplying the trucks and drivers that imported Canadian Whiskey to various cities, including Chicago. The elder Kennedy owned the largest building in Chicago (at the time), the Merchandise Mart. Although he became an ambassador to England, Joseph Kennedy was also a "bootlegger." The elder statesman was also involved in the motion picture industry and had a mistress, the actress Gloria Swanson.

As his son John Kennedy (his friends called him Jack) considered a major run for the presidency in 1960 (after a failed bid as vice-President on the Adlai Stevenson ticket in 1956), he was often introduced in a Vegas audience as "the senator from Massachusetts, Jack Kennedy" where Sinatra and the Rat Pack were performing at nightclubs.

The 1960 Presidential race against Richard Nixon was going to be a close one. Sinatra was actively campaigning for Kennedy and had re-recorded his popular song *High Hopes* with new lyrics about voting for Kennedy. Because of Peter Lawford and Frank Sinatra, Kennedy moved in many of the same circles of people. His younger brother, Robert, was his campaign manager, and they knew if they were going to win they had to have Illinois electoral votes. To get Illinois they had to have Chicago. The Democratic mayor, Mayor Richard Daley, had a good political machine but they had to be sure. Kennedy needed money so Sinatra asked a Chicago friend, Sam Giancana, head of the Chicago mob, for one million dollars. Giancana gave Kennedy the money he needed.

Were Giancana's motives as pure as helping his pal Frank? The feds were putting heat on mob operations and they needed a President that could steer the national agenda away from them.

By midnight of election night there was no clear-cut winner and Kennedy went to bed. Long after midnight many votes from the west side of Chicago that had been in the trunks of state troopers, and apparently took a long route, finally appeared. By the time all the votes came in, they put Kennedy over the top. He won Chicago, Illinois, and the country.

Sinatra was exuberant. He built a wing on his house for the President to stay during trips and also built a helicopter pad exclusively for the President to land. Sinatra got some of the biggest stars in Hollywood to come to Washington to perform for the inaugural ball including Sinatra himself.

All was going well until Kennedy announced that the new Attorney General would be his brother Robert Kennedy. That spelled trouble for the mob. Mom said to me, "This is not good (*non buono*). Never bite the hand that feeds you,"

During the late 1950s as counsel for a senate committee, Robert Kennedy had vigorously interrogated mob figures including Jimmy Hoffa of the Teamsters Union. The exchanges between Hoffa and Robert Kennedy, seen on live television, were so heated that one could see Hoffa seething with anger, if not hatred, as he left the Senate Hearing Room. Now RFK, the outspoken crusader against the mob, was the chief law enforcement prosecutor in the land.

My family sensed that Kennedy was in trouble. Although they supported him as a Catholic Democrat, my father said, "He's (Kennedy) got to remember who buttered his bread." Mom was more blunt, "You don't turn your back on Sinatra's friends. The vendetta *non dormire* (never sleeps)."

Frank Sinatra worked hard to get Kennedy elected President and was stunned when Robert Kennedy advised his brother to cut off relations. Sinatra was never invited to the White House. The President's helicopter never landed at Sinatra's helicopter pad nor would he ever stay in the wing Sinatra had built exclusively for him. One of the first things Robert Kennedy said was that his new agenda as

Attorney General was to "focus on destroying the crime syndicate and organized crime."

My parents saw Giancana's face contort whenever anyone mentioned the Kennedy name at his nightclub. My father knew Sam was not a guy to be crossed.

The anti-crime campaign got the mob's attention. In 1960 one of the first acts of the new Attorney General was to extradite (or rather kidnap) one of the most powerful mob bosses, Carlos Marcello of New Orleans. The Italians, New Orleans, and the mob had a long bond that went back to the 1880s. FBI agents literally grabbed Marcello off the street, handcuffed him, flew him in a private plane and dropped him off in a jungle in Guatemala. Marcello found his way back to America (with the help of his lawyer) and returned to New Orleans. He would never forget or forgive the insult.

Then a high-ranking lieutenant of a New York mob family named Joe Valachi agreed to go into the Federal Witness Protection Program and tell everything he knew about the mob. On live television, October 1963, he divulged the secret rite of initiation, *omerta* and the organizational structure of the mob. He named names. In the meantime, the FBI had wiretaps on the phones of key mob figures around the country. Hoffa, still seething from his run-ins with Bobby Kennedy, talked about someone placing a bomb under his car.

In referring to the Attorney General in conversation Marcello said, "A dog keeps biting if you only cut off its tail. You have to cut off the head."

Another mobster, Santos Trafficante of Miami, said, "He's going to be hit." Hoffa added, "He's got to go." The references seemed to apply to Robert Kennedy except for Marcello's comment about "cut off the head." The FBI knew something was going to happen but perhaps not where or when.

On November 22, 1963, a month after Valachi testified before the Senate, President Kennedy was assassinated in an open car in Dallas, Texas. My oldest brother Joseph said, "They got him." Who was "they?" Of course the official government version was a lone assassin named Lee Harvey Oswald. My brother had referred to a plural. My mother thought the President's death was a tragedy and mostly cried for the children. She also said, referring to Robert Kennedy, "He pushed 'them' too hard." By "them," she meant the mob.

The Warren Commission was quick to wrap everything into a tidy package of a disgruntled young lone assassin, like Zangera. There is little doubt that Oswald was present at the scene. But at best he was a marksman working with a poor Italian rifle that hardly worked in World War II. The wife of a police officer in my wedding party named Susan was a ballistics expert working at the FBI Washington crime lab in 1963. She was present when the gun was examined at FBI headquarters. "The sight was so out of alignment and the bolt action so sluggish you could have hardly hit a deer," she remarked to me, "We had to fix it before testing it."

Many people accepted the government's account as written in the Warren Commission. Mob connected family members never did. The country moved on to the escalation of the Vietnam War and civil rights, but under the Johnson and Nixon administration there was a significant justice department shift. In the first four years after the Kennedy assassination, there was a 72 percent **reduction** in justice department grand juries and trials against the mob. A mere coincidence?

Robert Kennedy was out of power for a time, serving as a senator from the State of New York. In that role, he was no danger to the mob. Then he ran for the presidency in 1968, and after a string of victories it became clear that he would receive the Democratic nomination in Chicago and had a good chance of being elected President. At his largest primary victory in California, he announced, "It's on to

Chicago." It was June 1968 and as he exited the Los Angeles hotel ballroom through the kitchen, lone assassin Sirhan Sirhan shot and killed him. Once again it was a clear cut, lone assassin explanation.

It turned out Sirhan Sirhan was a gambler at a local horse track and owed considerable debt to the mob. A last minute replacement as a security guard was a man named Thane Caesar, who had mob connections. The security guards that night carried .38s but Caesar also had a .22. People saw Caesar pull a gun supposedly to shoot at Sirhan, but Robert Kennedy was struck in the back of the head by a .22. There were a total of 13 bullets fired, although Sirhan's revolver only had a capacity for eight. In any great crime, you start with motive. Who would stand to gain? Who would want to kill Robert Kennedy?

The one category of criminal one rarely finds in prison is a *mob hit man*. They come in from another city, do their job and quickly exit. They are good at their work, and that is why they are rarely caught.

Who would fear Robert Kennedy becoming President the most? Was he prepared to open his brother's assassination investigation or start an aggressive agenda against the mob? People with a vendetta never forget.

While a great and exuberant leader, John Kennedy was known for some personal weaknesses, especially with women, as was his father. He was having an intimate relationship with a woman named Judith Campbell. She visited the White House on numerous occasions and there were 70 phone calls between her and Kennedy documented. Kennedy even made the mistake of writing her a personal check for $2,000 for her "services." The Rat Pack, especially brother-in-law Peter Lawford, knew of the affair. But even more, Judith Campbell was the mistress of Sam Giancana, the head of the Chicago mob. Sam did not take well to Kennedy using the powers and prestige of the Presidency to romance his own mistress. How did Kennedy meet Judith? Frank Sinatra introduced her to Jack Kennedy in Las Vegas.

Many have forgotten or simply lost interest in the reopening of the assassination investigation in March of 1978. The House Select Committee on Assassinations took another look at Kennedy's assassination. They found that a motorcycle policeman near Kennedy's limousine had a microphone stuck in the "on" position for at least 10 seconds. The sounds of the assassination were recorded on a dictabelt. Acoustical experts restaged the assassination but changed the positions of the gunfire to analyze the patterns. Rifle shots from the grassy knoll (a slight hill with a fence) matched those on the dictabelt.

Abraham Zapruder captured the assassination on 8mm film. He had his back to the fence. Most who have seen the digitally enhanced and slowed images come away with the impression that the fatal shot to Kennedy's right forehead would have perfectly matched someone with a rifle from behind the fence. The acoustical expert said, "There is a 95 percent or better odds that at least one shot came from the grassy knoll." From that point on, Lee Harvey Oswald became the "alleged" assassin. Three other facts have been strongly compelling to indicate who may have assassinated Kennedy.

1. Federal authorities wanted to know what Sam Giancana knew about the death of Kennedy, as well as involvement with the CIA regarding Fidel Castro. Sam was called to testify before a Senate Committee in 1975. The night before he was to leave for Washington, he was in his Oak Park apartment, and at least one friend was with him while he was grilling sausage on a skillet. As he attended to the cooking, he was shot in the back of the head with a .22. After falling to the ground, the assassin shot six more bullets under his chin and into his brain. There was no sign of forced entry. Giancana let the person or people in. The Sicilian style "hit" was unmistakable.

2. The next year, in 1976, Miami mobster John Roselli, also about to testify before the same committee, had already told the authorities that Jack Ruby was "one of our

boys." He disappeared. His dismembered body was found floating in an oil drum on Biscayne Bay in Miami.

3. Most compelling was Jack Ruby, the man who killed Lee Harvey Oswald. Who knows what information would have been gathered if Oswald had time to talk. Although he did talk to police the evening of the assassination and the following Saturday, there was no transcript or recording of what Oswald said. My family never believed Oswald carried off the assassination alone. Mom would say, "Ruby had to silence Oswald, just like Capone silenced people who knew too much."

The Warren Commission's explanation of Jack Ruby's act was that he wanted to spare the widow of Kennedy a trial. Although Oswald was one of the most protected suspects in one of the greatest crimes of the century, Ruby was able to walk into the police station and fire his gun right into Oswald's stomach, while each hand was held and restrained by police handcuffs. Ruby was a well known figure in Dallas, known to the Dallas police and the press. It was not considered unusual for him to be hanging around, especially at such a momentous time in history. Several police and news people commented on seeing him in the basement before the shooting.

Ruby knew Al Capone. His real name was Jack Rubenstein. He was from Chicago, and as a young gang member, a Chicago court declared him an "incorrigible delinquent." He was one of the young thugs that ran errands for Capone. He also hung around the lobby of the Sherman Hotel, one of Capone's headquarters, where he would act as a bookmaker and collect debts for Capone's brother Ralph and Frank Nitti.

Ruby collected dues for the Chicago chapter of the Teamster's Union between 1937 and 1940 and operated a string of strip joints in Chicago. He was involved in gambling, prostitution and drugs. His brother Hyman Rubenstein operated the Torch Club on Clark and Walter throughout the 1950s. In the back of the club were gaming tickets and illegal betting on horse races. Hymie was a professional gambler who ran a bookie joint. Since my father's employment was not far from the Torch Club and he used bookie joints frequently, it is likely he knew Rubenstein.

Jack Ruby did prison time for at least one murder and by all accounts committed several others. The Chicago mob wanted to move into Dallas and sent Ruby there in 1952. He opened two clubs including the Carousel Club at 1312 Commerce in Dallas. It was far more than a bar. It was a strip joint with prostitution, gambling and narcotics. Frequent guests at the Carousel Club included Dallas police. It was known that Jack made liberal payoffs and did many favors. It was said that of the 1,200 Dallas police in 1963, Jack Ruby knew the first names of 700, and they knew him.

The Warren Commission tried to establish Ruby as only a small time strip club owner. Yet his phone records showed extensive calls to Chicago, Miami and New Orleans. In 1959 he also visited the Tropicana Club in Havana, which was controlled by the mob. In the words of my brother Joseph, "Jack was a loyal soldier."

In news film of Ruby at police headquarters during a press conference on the night of November 22, he shouted out the correct name of Oswald's New Orleans affiliation, "Fair Play for Cuba," when a police captain got it wrong.

Who performed assassinations in America for one hundred years? Which assassins were rarely caught? Who had a strong motive for killing both Kennedy brothers? You decide. My family decided years ago.

About the time of Kennedy's death, it was time to take my place in the family "business." By my high school years I learned my family was not like my friend's families, especially the *Americans.* Our food was different, pasta and sauce (gravy) not hamburgers and ketchup. Our mannerisms were more demonstrative, especially the loud talking and broad hand gestures. While not every childhood friend had perfect parents, at least they were not constantly screaming and yelling at each other like mine.

Not all was negative, of course. My brother Anthony liked to entertain the family when he was a teenager. He would put on a silly hat and make an exaggerated clown face as the older relatives would roll with laughter. I enjoyed watching his performances.

My older brother Joseph was more serious and never seemed to have time or patience for his little brother Donnie, so Anthony was saddled with me at my mother's insistence. I remember him holding my hand and taking me to the Saturday matinees at the Montclair movie theater. We would see Martin and Lewis and Abbott and Costello movies for fifty cents.

Anthony was more fun. When I was thirteen, I borrowed my father's 8mm camera. In the backyard Anthony and I produced short comedies. I was the cameraman and Anthony was the actor. They were sophomoric: a series of pratfalls, a pie in the face, even Anthony sinking into quicksand. Our mother deplored that scene since she couldn't find her boxes of oatmeal. We dug a pit in the backyard, filled it with water and then oats. She did not understand how we could be eating so much oatmeal until the day we premiered the film for the family. When she saw the pit and my brother fall into it, she exclaimed, "So that's where all my packages have been going!" Mom never let us forget it. She would tell that story hundreds of times, partly for sympathy, but also to show others how clever and funny her boys were.

Because we shared the same bedroom, I remember Anthony coming in well after midnight with the strong smell of alcohol on his breath and cigarette smoke in his clothes, talking about the Club Hollywood. This was a local nightclub where aspiring entertainers and occasionally famous celebrities performed. I could only imagine the world of the nightclub, having never been in one. He didn't go into details but implied sexual escapades with one girl after another. Anthony kept a small black book, which I looked through one day. There were over 40 girls' names, each with a one-line comment about physical attributes or personality. Anthony had the image in school (even junior high) of a playboy. He slicked his hair back with pomade into a ducktail, rolled up his shirtsleeves to show his biceps, and wore tight straight-legged khakis and penny loafers. He usually had a cigarette hanging from the corner of his mouth, like James Dean.

Surprisingly, this image did not bother my parents. My father was a heavy smoker. When he sent me to the local Rexall drugstore for cigarettes it was for a carton of Chesterfields, never a pack. My mother was also a smoker. She would meet other neighborhood women in the early morning around our kitchen table for what she called "a coffee klotch." They would play cards, gossip, and of course eat pastries and drink coffee. It was amazing to watch them, mostly with curlers in their hair and cigarettes hanging from their mouths. This was the early 50s, and Lucy and Desi smoked, too. So they had no problem with my brother's smoking.

As a boy I would get into my brother's entertainment act. I would perform magic tricks and being the smallest, would go into a box and disappear through a "secret" trap door. The family would applaud as if mesmerized by the very visible trick.

I remember large tables with 30 relatives having an elaborate meal. There were separate tables for the children, often card tables in other rooms. When the parties were large, the family would put plywood planks on sawhorses draped with white tablecloths in basements and garages. Meals would last three to four hours with breaks between courses for conversation, the smoking of a fine cigar and even an occasional nap. After dinner, the smell of garlic lingered in the air. I remember everyone talked loudly. To an "American" visitor it would seem as if everyone was fighting, but that was just the way we talked. Sicilians made their points with volume and they had no rules against interrupting each other in mid-sentence. An argument could erupt over the most miniscule fact. Which grocer had the better tomatoes? Who made the best soup? Which ballroom had the best band? Who played better accordion, Connie Francis or Dick Contino? Who had the better voice, Jerry Vale or Al Martino? There was rarely an argument over Tony Bennett versus Frank Sinatra; however, it was always Sinatra, hands down.

A non-Italian in our home at mealtime would have been confused, mistaking early courses for the main course. We would feast on zucchini topped with mozzarella cheese, eggplant deep fried in olive oil with parsley, huge bowls of spaghetti with a rich meat sauce the family called "gravy," ample Marsala wine in the familiar straw casing, and Italian bread often twisted with an egg on top, especially at Easter. As if that was not enough, next came a large salad with oil and vinegar dressing. It was the Italian custom to eat the salad last, not as the Americans do at the beginning. But in this respect, my family had become "Americanized." During the rest period, which could last an hour, the relatives cracked nuts and ate grapes and dates. Next, the women would put out huge platters of meat: chicken, roast beef, veal scaloppini. There was never an option not to take food. The cook would be insulted if you did not try everything. *"Maugiare,"* was the word of the day, "eat, eat." After the last break would come platters of Sicilian pastry, cannoli (fried pastry filled with ricotta cheese and flavored with wine, candied fruit and powdered sugar) and home-baked cookies with Amaretto.

There was never any talk of *business* at the dinner table: the gunning down of a local merchant, running numbers, or placing a bet on the seventh at Arlington. These conversations were considered inappropriate, even profane. "Business" was kept outside of the home. The home was for family.

My favorite family memories revolved around food and eating but also music. The last fond memory of my brothers came when I was in my late twenties. Anthony was in his mid-thirties and Joseph was turning forty. After a good meal, Anthony would select a vinyl LP of an opera (from my mother's collection) and play it. Then pretending we all knew Italian, we would begin singing along opera style with the famed tenor or baritone on the record. I remember the laughter. We would sing with abandonment. My mother would laugh and say, "That's not Italian. You don't know what you're singing." But she would continue laughing. The younger children would try to mimic us. Each of us, Joseph, Anthony and younger brother Donnie, would take turns with operatic solos. We were terrible, of course, but if one did not know better, they would think we actually knew what we were singing. Sometimes I would laugh so hard I could feel the veins expanding on my temples. I would have tears stream from my eyes from the laughter. I miss those moments. I remember Joseph's broad smile and Anthony laughing until his face turned bright red. How did a family that had so much fun together become so silent, solemn, and split apart?

Joseph was always more "dago" than Anthony. My brother Joseph was 6'4" with black wavy hair. He dressed up in fine tailored silk suits, often silver, gray or black. Most of the time he wore silk dress pants, black leather shoes and expensive polo shirts. Joseph also wore a little gold crucifix next to a gold Italian horn on his neck. He always had a pinkie ring with a large diamond as well as other rings, an expensive watch, a gold bracelet and a thick gold chain. When he dressed down, he would simply wear a black leather jacket. Like my father, he wore dress hats, hundred dollar hats with slightly creased brims.

There were telltale signs of hidden lives, but I had to look closely to see them. By my teens, both older brothers had cars. I frequently noticed a small wooden club under the driver's seat of each auto.

I learned not to ask questions because the answers were usually evasive, such as:

"What's the club for?" I'd ask.

"An emergency," Anthony responded.

"What kind of emergency?" I inquired.

"In case of trouble," came the snap answer.

They never elaborated. When Anthony was older and living in his beauty shop, he began to carry a gun. It was concealed, but I caught a glimpse now and then. It looked like a .357 magnum. All I know was, it was large. By then I learned not to ask. The answers would have been evasive, anyway. The gun made me suspicious.

Something happened my first day of high school that aroused my suspicions further about the kind of people my brothers were. My guidance counselor selected classes in the industrial arts; woodworking, metals, electricity and leather shop. I guess no one thought I had any college potential. Dad didn't even challenge the counselor. No one in my family had a college degree, yet had fine clothes and possessions, so why make the effort. Dad never finished high school

I was seated at a table the first day of leather class, and the teacher, Mr. Zingrabe, a man with short gray hair and small black eyes, without any warning, hit me in the back of the head with a hammer. I turned in absolute shock. He exclaimed angrily, "This is if you are anything like your brothers!" It was not a metal hammer; but a small wood and leather hammer used to put marks in a belt or a wallet. It hurt nonetheless. I never told my brothers the teacher had hit me and for good purpose. I didn't like the teacher, but I didn't think he deserved a broken arm, either.

By the time I got to high school both brothers were long gone but had left a trail of bad memories with all the teachers and especially the dean. The East Leyden High School Dean of Men, Mr. Morehausen, a bald, short man with blue eyes, called me to his office one day and said,

"I'm looking forward to a good year. I don't want any trouble." I was confused. "Your brothers gave me nothing but grief," he continued, "I don't want another four years of that!"

I was starting to build a mental image of what my brothers had really been like in school; chronically late, truant, disruptive, smoking, fighting and sexually promiscuous. As I started the school year, Anthony and Joseph said to me separately, "If anybody gives you any trouble, you tell me and I'll handle it." I began to tie that message to the club under the car seat. I realized I had the power to put a teacher in a cast just by naming him. Even when I had a problem, I never went to my brothers, fearing that the reaction would be far more extreme than my problem. It could be a shattered kneecap or a broken arm. As a freshman, several older thugs took my lunch money from time to time. I never said a word.

My brothers had a bond I could never infiltrate. It was not the traditional sibling rivalry I felt. It was more the notion that Joseph was schooling Anthony and I was not part of the class.

I was in junior high when a physical fight broke out between my father and my oldest brother Joseph because of his behavior. Joseph would come home at three and four a.m. after a night of drinking and gambling. He was playing cards and gambling on bowling matches. My father kept a small wooden chest in his closet. It was not very secure, but to him it was a safe where he kept extra cash and papers. My father discovered that Joseph had broken in with a screwdriver and stolen money to gamble with. I vividly remember the fight. My father was threatening him verbally. As my brother Joseph tried to enter the house, my father was pressing the door against his arm. My mother was crying and screaming, "Marty you're going to hurt him!"
Then Dad gave Joseph an ultimatum, "You're going into the army or you're going to jail."

Soon after, my brother enlisted in the navy, but my mother continued in her role as enabler. He was gambling on the ship, a destroyer, the USS DeHaven and she was wiring him money via Western Union without my father's knowledge.

Joseph picked up a girl, Betty, in a San Diego bar, brought her home and announced he would marry her.

My mother was shocked. Betty was thoroughly American, not a drop of Italian blood. The only redeeming fact was her brother was a Carmelite priest. They got married, but within weeks arguments erupted that escalated from the verbal to the physical. She hit him with a pie one day. I'm not sure what his retaliation was. I can only imagine. They would pull in front of our house on a Sunday afternoon and sit in the car for what seemed like an hour yelling at each other. My mother would watch nervously through the blinds of the kitchen window. The new wife was spending her afternoons at a local bar and after three months took a plane back to southern California.

The next time, Joseph picked an Italian girl from a good Italian neighborhood. This pleased my mother. But they could not get married in the church because of his divorce, yet a little money soon greased church authority for a Vatican annulment, meaning the marriage was never consummated.

Many afternoons as a teen I would visit Joseph at his barbershop. The small town of Stone Park was where Capone had owned much real estate. Most of his customers were thugs and hoodlums. They were also racists who would beat to a pulp any black man that dared to walk the streets of Stone Park or Melrose Park after dark. Looking at an Italian woman would get you shot and dumped in a ditch.

Mom was crying one evening. She was upset that Joseph, now out of the navy, was in legal trouble. He had been dealing in gold coins with a business partner. Mom said,

"He's meeting with Thompson, the State's Attorney." The business partner had fled to Las Vegas and Joseph was given an ultimatum to cooperate or go to prison. Thompson would become the future governor of Illinois. My mother's take was that Joseph was innocent, of course. This proved to be only the *tip of the iceberg* in terms of my brothers' behavior. For Joseph and Anthony, I was considered next in line.

I was depressed

I was depressed.

I was depressed but didn't share it with anyone.

Growing up, I was carefully taught that *depression* was not something our family talked about. And I really did not know I was depressed since I thought I had conquered my anger problem and had gotten control of it rather than it controlling me.

What I didn't realize was that I had turned all my anger on myself and it had turned into depression, a depression so deep and so dark it threatened my own life.

Giving my life to the Church was sincere and I really hoped to save my family from eternal damnation. But while the setting of the Benedictine monastery was a tranquil place, the appearance of being religious brought no peace to my soul. I was play-acting. I would wear religious garments and do good things, not only to get myself in heaven but my family as well. But the good acts never felt like enough. There always seemed something more I had to do to gain God's approval. It felt like a religious treadmill, a lot of energy going nowhere.

I would pray for a "happy death" everyday as a youth: time for an act of contrition and the last rites, fearing that if I died suddenly I would go straight to hell. Every Mafia hoodlum gunned down but with minutes of life left would "go to heaven if a priest reached him in time and anointed his head with holy oil," my mother would teach me.

One late night walking out in a cornfield behind the monastery, I realized (by the power of the Holy Spirit) that I was a sinner and Christ had paid the price for my sins. The experience was like a blindness being lifted from my eyes. I began to read Scriptures as if for the first time.

But I knew so little about reformation history I thought everyone would be happy for me. Immediately it put me at odds with church leaders, the abbot and my bishop. I hid my family background from them, yet in many ways a bishop could be like a family *capo*, at least the ones I knew. My bishop, Romeo Blanchette, said to me one day, dressed elaborately in scarlet and holding the emerald studded pectoral cross he wore, "Stop reading the Bible! It is getting you in trouble. We will interpret it for you."

I disobeyed him.

It never crossed my mind to leave the Roman Catholic Church initially. After all, it was part of my Italian culture. Major family events were entwined with the church; the celebration of infant baptism, first communion, and confirmation. It was never as simple as saying "I'll become a Presbyterian or a Baptist."

For the longest time I believed I could reform the church. At one point I was going to start my own religious order. A wiser priest, Father Francis Filas, a Jesuit, said, "Roman!"

I did not understand. "This is not just the Catholic Church, it is the Roman Catholic Church and it has a history of control that goes back centuries," the priest elaborated.

I thought he was being rude, but I now look back and realize he was giving me sound advice. I was not going to change this great monolith with a history of canonization, papal encyclicals, papal infallibility, and a rigid hierarchy. But it was possible I could remain and be lost myself in a world of pharisee-ism. I feared that more.

Leaving was not an easy transition. I attended mass every day. I studied in the seminary for over seven years. I was ordained a cleric. Above all, Mom was so proud to have a son who was a priest.

As a child, nuns would drill us with the catechism "the Roman Catholic Church is the one true church."

Do not misunderstand. I have many friends in the Roman Catholic Church who know Jesus and are totally saved. But for me personally, it was a step I felt I had to take. I did not want to see Jesus through a thick wall of man-made rules and church law.

In the back of my mind there was a tiny voice that kept saying, "What if you are wrong? What if it is the true church?" And harder still, I had to break the news to my mother. She was disappointed but continued to pray for me each day.

When I left the monastery, I met a godly man; a pastor from the largely Italian community of Melrose Park named John Marchese. He gave me a key to his small Bible church, a church where my future wife's grandmother had attended after breaking with tradition in the 1940s.

The Italian Catholics looked down on the Bible Church. In previous years they would walk to the other side of the street, not even looking at the building, and sometimes throw rotten fruit and eggs. Italians can be dramatic. This was the town of the Feast of the Madonna. To break from the Catholic Church was considered sinful and would bring the loss of eternal salvation.

With the key to the Bible Church building, I would enter late at night, sometimes after midnight and by the faintest light from a streetlight through a colored window, seek God's guidance.

I did embrace many of the traditions of the Roman Catholic Church; pipe organ music, Gregorian chant, the use of the arts in stained glass windows and solemn rituals that included holding the Bible aloft while processing down the center aisle. Clearly the Roman Catholic Church was the church from the time of Christ. Anyone who studies church history also knows what happened during the Dark Ages. The Bible was forbidden to be written in the common language or read by the average person. Most Christians were uneducated and taught about indulgences, the worship of saints, including the various apparitions of the Virgin Mary. Through the centuries corrupt bishops and popes clearly veered from the simple message of Christ.

I had been taught by Jesuit professors that the Reformation was "a movement started by devils," that Martin Luther, John Knox, John Calvin, Ulrich Zwingli and Michael Sattler were writhing in hell because of their rejection of Roman Catholic authority and theology.

Leaving the Roman Catholic Church was the first major break from my upbringing, tradition and culture. It was more a process than a decision on any given day. I stopped going to mass, instead attending services in charismatic churches. I was most fortunate to meet a wonderful Italian woman, Regina, who would become my wife. Her mother Gloria was raised an Italian in Melrose Park but a Bible believing woman with a strong faith.

Before meeting my wife, I went through a spiral of dark depression. I wanted to be a priest but for all the wrong reasons. I knew in my heart that I had no calling to celibacy. It was a long and winding journey that took me from the Joliet Diocese to a Benedictine monastery to the Rockford Diocese, the Paulist Order and finally the Scalabrini Order where I was within months of full ordination.

The break was not only from the church of my youth but a break with family. My mother was devastated. She still clung to the statues that I had given her and the prayers to saints that I had taught her.

"You can go back," she said tearfully, "the church needs you."

"There are other ways to serve God," I told her.

Anthony continued as an atheist, wavering with agnosticism, but Joseph was a ritualistic Catholic who would pin money to the costume of the statue Our Lady of Mt. Carmel that processed through the streets, and his wife would shuffle on her knees in the procession. These were devout people.

At funerals and family events, older relatives would whisper behind my back, "He was the one who was a priest." Oddly, no one ever asked me why I left. I wanted to explain my newfound faith but there was a closed mentality.

After my father's death and the uncovering of so much secrecy, I became angrier about my family. Rather than smashing glasses and hitting people, all the anger was turned inside and it developed into a dark depression.

I was lonely and hardly dating, would see a late night movie then sit in an all night diner until one or two in the morning reading a book. I was living back with my mother and when I would return home, she would say, "I was worried. I thought you were in a ditch." Throughout my youth she always talked about a "ditch" she thought my brothers and I were in as a result of an auto accident when we came home late.

Wanting independence but not being able to afford to move out was difficult.

One time Mom, waking up late, said, "I know what young men do."

I responded, "I don't understand."

She said, "I know what young men do late at night with the money they offer women."

I couldn't believe it. My mother actually thought I was with prostitutes when, in fact, I was doing my best to lead a good, moral life. That judgment made me sad.

It was during this period my oldest brother Joseph became angry with me. At Christmas I would choose to stay at home, alone. I would read the Christmas narrative in the Bible, pray, and enjoy contemplating the Savior' birth. The parties at Joseph's home were raucous with an abundance of booze, inebriated people, a cloud of cigarette smoke and a focus on materialism. A part of the monastery atmosphere was still in me, and my new faith, although barely an ember, was growing.

Joseph would phone and call me names. "You're an idiot," he would say. "What's wrong with you?"

I guess I had not learned the social custom of just showing up for a while and then leaving. By boycotting family events, Joseph was getting more exasperated with me. The comments after my father's funeral were only the tip of the iceberg.

In those days, we were all good Chicago Democrats. When I mentioned I was going to vote for a Republican, Joseph exploded, "Are you a Communist?" As *padrone* (boss) of the family, he felt his role was to keep everyone in line. To have broken from the Roman Catholic Church, and to have not voted for a Chicago Democrat, were unimaginable breaks with tradition.

I purchased a small black revolver. Everyone in the family had some kind of weapon. One day I was sitting in a room in the back of our house next to the bar where I had labored as a child bartender. I was alone. I was contemplating suicide. I looked at the gun, checked to see that a bullet was in every chamber then raised it to my head. I kept my hand tightly gripped with my finger on the trigger, thinking about my choices. One of the choices was ending my life.

I could not imagine life getting better. I wished that I had been able to talk to a professional counselor. If I had talked to someone in junior high, high school, or in college and not given the traditional answer of "fine," I may have been able to deal with the source of my anger. But now it was full blown depression. I felt a dark spiral that was pulling me in. I did not feel the love of my family. I was tired of peeling back, layer by layer, family secrets. I sat looking at that gun for over four hours. My mother was at Joseph's home at the time.

Finally I made a decision not to end my life, removed the bullets from the chambers and put the gun away. I never held the gun again in that way. I was not trying to be dramatic, since no one knew I did it, and I never told anyone until many years later when I was giving a chapel address at Wheaton College.

Christians, after all, "are never depressed," some would say. Such comments often isolate people who are feeling depression. "It must be a weakness of faith," or "If you had a strong faith, you would never be depressed; others would say." I do not believe that. I believe Christians can be angry and depressed just like anyone else. My faith was not strong enough at the time to rely on the power of God. But I know it was God that kept me from killing myself with that revolver.

My marriage to Regina was one of the best things that ever happened in my life. She was and is a beautiful Christian woman, and after my marriage, my depression simply faded away. I had needed love in my life, and it replaced the vacuum I had long felt in my family.

As a young Christian, I had an erroneous theory. I believed that everyone has suffering, and that somehow it is measured and everyone has an equal dose.

When our son Luke was born, it was one of the happiest days of my life. Having committed myself to a life of celibacy, it is difficult to explain in words what it felt like when God gave me the gift of a son. I sang at the top of my voice as I drove from the hospital that Saturday evening.

Three months later when he was in heart failure and rushed to a hospital about to have open-heart surgery, I found it difficult to understand. Joseph offered to pay for a second opinion at Mayo Clinic, but we were at one of the finest children's hospitals in the country. Yet Dr. Idriss, an accomplished pediatric heart surgeon, felt that the odds were against us. The team of surgeons had never attempted to correct the combination of heart problems and defects our son had.

Even though I had been a professional cleric and had worn religious garments for many years, when I sat in the tiny hospital chapel the night before surgery, I could not find the words to pray. God, of course, knew my heart.

I simply walked up to the altar and struck it with my fist. I was angry at God, yet did not want to say the words. I struggled with my own feeling of powerlessness. Then with the smallest thread of faith, trusted God. After eight hours of surgery there was a risk of brain damage, but after ten hours the surgeon came out. Dr. Idriss said, "That was one of the most difficult surgeries I have ever performed." As he walked away, he suddenly turned and said, "I felt as if there was an angel in the operating room guiding my hand."

I soon found suffering is not measured in equal doses. At 18 months of age, Luke began to wind down like a machine wearing out. It was time for another open-heart surgery, but I had lost my job and had no medical insurance. We had over $130,000 in medical bills. Again, by God's grace, our son came through the surgery, but it had a tremendous effect on my wife and me.

Unable to afford a Chicago hotel, we were grateful to stay at the Ronald McDonald House for $5 a night. We lived with other parents whose children had leukemia, heart disease and other illnesses. We had been drawn into a world we did not know existed. We comforted parents who lost their children. After surgery, while Luke was in intensive care, we would literally sleep on vinyl couches. One time, Regina and I literally forgot to eat for three days, only drinking cups of coffee.

At this time, I started a film company. I had been successful producing documentary films, but it was easier to be a free-lance cinematographer when single. To meet the monthly demand of bills, I went from one job to another until an opportunity opened to work in the court system with juveniles.

I could tell that both Anthony and Joseph always looked down on my work in the court system, but I never knew why. I found that I had a gift for working with troubled adolescents, and it was more than a job, it was the beginning of a career, if not a calling.

Joseph was always trying to recommend other jobs for me like selling cars or selling insurance. It all had to do with money. "You will never make any money doing that," Joseph would say, referring to my work in the justice system.

Joseph felt judges and police were people you "bribed" when you needed their help. He had no respect for the law, just ways of "getting by" and "around" and "acquiring" stolen merchandise for gifts, not unlike my father.

I would still have bad days and get down from time to time, but I was no longer depressed.

If my being a priest made my brothers uncomfortable, my being a court officer brought strong disapproval. Someday I would discover why.

I was suspicious

I was suspicious.

I was suspicious my brothers were deeply involved in crime. There were so many indications and signs you would've had to be blind to miss it. But in many ways I was still naïve, thinking the best of my family, especially my brothers. Yet the patterns, like those of early ancestors, were building.

The height of my suspicion came on Sunday, April 19, 1981. It was Easter and the family was having dinner at my brother Anthony's house. As often happened, I walked into a room where Anthony and Joseph were talking and they abruptly stopped, turned and looked at me.

"Don't let me interrupt," I said, "Continue." But as long as I stood there, they said nothing. I was uneasy, so I turned and left the room. Anthony got up and closed the door, yet I could hear muffled voices as their conversation continued.

Later that afternoon, the whole family was sitting in Anthony's living room. There had been a lot of body language and eye contact between my brothers. I saw Anthony look over to Joseph. Simultaneously they stood up, walked to the front closet and put on long overcoats. Anthony turned to me and said, " Come, walk with us."

My mother immediately chimed in, "*Andare a spasso.* (Go for a walk.) I like to see the brothers together."

The air was cold, the sun had just gone down, and a brisk wind stirred, so I really didn't want to be walking outside. I was flanked on either side by my brothers. Yet no one said a word. We walked nearly two blocks to a vacant stretch of undeveloped land populated by overgrown weeds.

Anthony began, "You know we care about you," he said.

I nodded my head.

"Joe and I had good luck in business recently," Anthony continued, "we want to share our success with you."

Joseph remained silent as we walked. Then Anthony said, "It's time for you to come in business with us."

"I've had a recent promotion and the chief judge likes me," I responded, but Joseph barked, "*E chi se ne frega*? (Who gives a damn?) That means nothing!"

Anthony continued, calming Joseph, "We're talking about real money here, money that can buy a big house, a boat and cars."

I interjected, "That doesn't mean anything to me. I want to do something good with my life."

Anthony cut me off in mid-sentence, "We have something for you."

At that comment, we stopped walking. Joseph patted the outside of his coat as Anthony said, "This is for you." Joseph reached inside his coat pocket as my heart beat faster. I quickly scanned the horizon. No one was in sight. The sky darkened. I was feeling *muscled*. Then Joseph pulled out a thick envelope, handing it to Anthony who, in turn, handed it to me. I took it but did not open the envelope, intuitively knowing the contents.

"We're giving you $50,000 to come in with us." Anthony declared, "You're holding $20,000. The other 30's in the car." My mind raced. A car salesman and a hairdresser, where did they get so much money?

After holding it for less than a minute, I handed the envelope back to Anthony. Joseph erupted, "*Cafone!* (Idiot!)" I began shaking from the chill of the wind as the conversation had taken on a cold tone.

Both brothers stared angrily at me.

"You don't get it!" Joseph blurted, "The money's yours, right now."

"*Famiglia*," Anthony intoned in Italian. "Family, that's all that matters."

We circled back toward the house. Before entering, we stopped and Anthony said, "This is between us."

Joseph added, "We never had this conversation." I looked at him. "*Capice?*" he said sternly, which means *understand*.

I didn't answer.

Under his breath Joseph said, "*Non dire mai nulla a nessuno.* (Don't ever say anything to anybody.)"

I shared the conversation with my wife on the long drive home. The family (my brothers) was *borgata*, a crime family. If I took the money I would be *il crimine con mio fratelli,* involved in a way of life without an exit. Of course, I could have used the money as the bills from my son's heart surgeries were growing, but I also valued integrity. Every time I took an oath to tell the truth before a judge as an officer of the court, I had the trust of the attorneys and the judge. A year earlier I may have easily rationalized taking it because of the need for money. Only the grace of God gave me the strength to resist going into the family "business."

Simply don't ask questions, keep the money hidden, and don't tell your wife was the pattern of my family going back many years. As I looked back, the puzzle pieces started to come together.

It began almost ten years earlier in 1972 after the release of the successful film *The Godfather.* My brother Anthony started insisting that family members refer to him as the "godfather." It seemed a joke, but he was serious. Anthony had an influence over his older brother Joseph in the way the fictional character Michael Corleone had over his older brother Fredo. If Anthony was like *The Godfather* character, then it fit that there were secretive, closed-door conversations much earlier.

Another puzzle piece came in the person of a man from Germany. In 1967 Anthony had a business partner named Fritz, a jovial, overweight man with an infectious laugh, who was a business partner with Anthony in the Velvet Brush Beauty Parlor in Deerfield, Illinois. Fritz was an expert hairdresser and loved to gossip with the ladies. Fritz became a family friend and an "uncle" to me. He was invited to all the family parties. A German citizen, he spoke in a thick accent. Holding a mug of beer, he enjoyed the Italian songs my mother would sing, often singing along.

One day, my brother Anthony had a pain in the calf of a leg. It turned out to be phlebitis (a blood clot) and it was the doctor's instructions that Anthony keep his leg elevated. My mother fretted over his illness. Anthony turned over the day-to-day responsibilities of the beauty shop to Fritz. Several times I saw his partner stop by with the financial books accounting for the week's receipts.

One day Anthony slammed down the book in front of my older brother Joseph. Watching television in another room, I am confident they did not think I was listening or understood. *"Sporco Porco*! (Dirty pig!) He's skimming!" Anthony exclaimed to Joseph. Then as my mother approached the room, they quieted down.

Anthony returned to the beauty shop after a few weeks but told my mother, "Fritz decided to go back to Germany."

"So quickly?" my mother asked.

It did not make any sense to me. He had been a family friend. "Why would he leave without saying goodbye?" I asked my mother.
"I don't know," she quietly answered, looking to the floor.

Later we were at a family party and I overheard Joseph say to Anthony, *"Ecco il gionmale.* (Here is the newspaper.) Too bad, too bad." Anthony murmured as he glanced at a newspaper article, *"Peggio per lui.* (Serves him right.)"

They went to the basement where drinks were being served. I picked up the newspaper. "Man Found Dead" the caption read with Fritz's first and last name. He had been killed in the style of a "hit." Moreover, he had been dismembered; his remains wrapped in newspaper and put in the trunk of his own automobile abandoned in a parking lot. My mother simply said, *"Succedono tante cose tristi.* (So many sad things happen.) We live in a terrible world," and just shook her head.

I had thought that Fritz and Anthony were close, at least as business partners. They drank and laughed together, and yet Anthony did not seem shocked by the news. This was another side of my brother I had never seen, no real emotions. Anthony called Fritz a *ruffiano*, which is Sicilian slang for *trash* or *low class*.

When I pressed Anthony for a motive for the death, Joseph half whispered, "*Meno si dice, meglione´*. (The less you say, the better) to Anthony."

"Who would have wanted to kill poor Fritz?" I asked myself. Not thinking the conversation between Anthony and Joseph were in any way related to his disappearance or violent death, I put this incident in the back of my mind.

I was married in 1976. I had a traditional Italian wedding with a large wedding party of twelve, over 350 guests, and an elaborate dinner at a four-star hotel. My grandfather's brother Filippo led the "grand march" followed by the tarantella, a wild dance that imitated being bit by a black widow spider in our native region of Sicily.

The night before my wedding, Joseph and Anthony took me out for dinner. At another table in the restaurant was Watergate prosecutor Albert Jenner. Anthony called the waiter and said, "Send that table your best bottle of wine." I watched him write a note, "Thank you for what you are doing in America by fighting crime." It was a moment of intense pride for me. My brother was breaking ranks with the family traditions of crime by honoring a crime fighter.

Both Anthony and Joseph were in the wedding party the next day and Anthony was my best man. As was tradition, he stood up, and offered my wife and me a toast, "*Salute!* (To your health!)," "*Longevita!* (Long life!)" and "*Felicita!* (Happiness!)"

We came back from the honeymoon and I bought my wife a Schnauzer puppy for her birthday. I stopped by Anthony's beauty shop, The Velvet Brush, to show him the dog. It was a large shop with many operators. The women workers enjoyed playing with the puppy.

My brother was busy with a client when one of the employees asked me, "Is Anthony all right?" I was confused. A few of the other employees were concerned about him as well. She gestured for me to follow her down the hall. It was mysterious. She brought me to what had previously been the men's washroom. When I opened the door, I saw a rocking chair, an end table with a lamp and a magazine rack on a circular carpet, all neatly positioned. Against one wall was an army cot. There was a pipe resting on an ashtray on a table. In every other way, this small room was a restroom, complete with a urinal on the wall and a toilet in a metal stall. On the shelf over the restroom sink were Anthony's comb, toothbrush, mouthwash and electric shaver.

"Your brother lives here," she said resoundingly. I was surprised. That moment confirmed for me that my brothers and I lived in two different worlds. The gulf between us had done nothing but increase over the years.

Secrets continued. No one had told me, including my mother, that Anthony had divorced his wife a week before our wedding. Anthony was becoming more of a mystery. At a family party the next year my mother said to him, "You keep changing. One day your hair is long, the next day it is short and curly. You had a beard last month, last week only a mustache and now you're clean-shaven. Why do you keep changing your appearance?" Anthony made a joke of it and everyone laughed. His changes of appearance were dramatic, however, and made me wonder.

It was the first time our son Luke had gone outside our home since his second open-heart surgery in March 1979. It was a Fourth of July party at Joseph's house and Anthony arrived with a cast on his arm.

"What happened?" my wife asked Anthony.

"I was playing tennis and pulled a muscle," he responded

I was not aware he played tennis. In the living room, one of his sons was looking through a book of architectural designs of homes.

"What are you looking at?" I asked my nephew.

"My dad's going to build us a big home. Look at this one," my nephew pointed to a stone structure of 6,000 square feet with arches and multiple chimneys.

Later that year, Anthony bought a new sports car. Joseph was also doing well materially. Although officially only selling cars, he had built an enormous lake home with a waterfront pier and a motorboat, as well.

After the offer of the $50,000 there were other mysterious signs. The secret conversations increased. At family gatherings, I would walk into a room and they would abruptly stop talking. Other times I would catch them glance at each other, stand simultaneously, put their coats on and leave. The wives and my mother would comment that the brothers were "getting closer." But the longer this behavior went on, the more it seemed odd. One day I heard that they had met on the shoulder of a toll road, secretive and strange behavior.

My brothers were making plans for something big, under safe conditions. People in crime avoid what is called "hot places," any location under surveillance. My brothers did not even talk by phone. To avoid hidden recording devices, they would walk and talk and pat people on the back as if frisking them when greeting them.

Then the trips began. It started innocently. In October 1981 my mother called to wish me a happy birthday. She added, "Your brother Tony would have called but he's in California." I knew that Anthony went to California frequently and asked what he was doing.

She simply said, "business." When I asked what kind of business, she said defensively, "How would I know!?" I asked why someone who owned a beauty shop would go to California every couple of weeks. She became irritated.

"You're trying to put me on the spot," Mom said, "It's something I'm not supposed to talk about."

At that point I realized there was something she knew (and perhaps other family members knew) that I did not know. I was annoyed. My mother often scolded me for not being closer to my brothers and yet here was a classic example of them shutting me out.

"Is he selling drugs?" I questioned, hardly daring to ask.

My mother exploded, "How could you ever think such a thing of your brother? He would never do anything dishonest."

The trips to California were to start a "chain of tanning parlors," she confided.

"Why California with all that sun?" I thought to myself.

The travels increased. One week he went to London where, according to my mother, he was studying with Vidal Sassoon. Both brothers traveled to Amsterdam, Paris, Berlin and Geneva. Then Anthony bragged one evening at a family party, now with long hair and a full beard, that he had a romance with a Russian ballerina. I could not tell if it was fantasy or reality.

Several months later Joseph and Anthony went to the Middle East. They told the family how they had gone to a de-militarized zone and were stopped at gunpoint by the PLO. The family, especially their children, was amused by these adventures. But how were the trips funded? Anthony was a hairdresser. Joseph was a barber selling cars. Did they have a secret life?

The phone rang very early September 4, 1982. It was my brother Joseph. "Get over here immediately," he said. (I lived 20 miles away.) It was 7:30 a.m. I concluded there had been a terrible accident or someone had died.

"What is it?" I asked.

"Just get here!" Joseph bellowed.
I had time to call my mother-in-law Gloria, a prayer warrior. "There must have been an accident or a death," I told her and asked her to pray. When I got to his house, his wife ushered me into the den. I must have seemed anxious, yet they chatted initially about the weather and other matters. They were both relaxed.

Finally Joseph said, "Our brother Tony was arrested for trespassing in a bank."

"Anthony arrested?" I reacted with shock.

His wife Marie shook her head in disbelief. "We don't know why he was there," Joseph continued, "but he was taken to the Lake County Jail, then bonded out. Last night he was in our backyard crying like a baby."

Joseph's wife went into the kitchen to make coffee. When she left, Joseph leaned toward me and said, "Remember that walk we had outside?" I could not recall. He continued, "Remember the offer of $50,000?"

"Yes," I replied.

"Well, you can see how that could look now. The FBI is trying to pin all sorts of unsolved cases on Tony and it could look bad. Remember," he said dramatically, "*Famiglia!* Family comes before everything. We <u>never</u> had that conversation!"

Then Joseph reached for the phone, dialed and said, "Tony, your brother Donnie is sitting here, he wants to help you. Talk to him." He handed the phone over to me. I did not know what to say. It was awkward, as I was not prepared to talk with Anthony. Joseph took back the phone and nodded as Anthony talked.

Joseph and his wife walked me to the door. Over the years I had been graciously entertained in their home many times for holidays, their boy's birthdays and special gatherings. His wife Marie had a gift for hospitality. Yet I did not know as I was leaving that morning that I would never set foot in that house again. I had no idea of what was unfolding.

A few days later I met with Anthony. "Get me a psychiatrist I can visit," he ordered. (At the court I worked with several psychiatrists.)

"Can you tell me what happened?" I responded.

Anthony glared at me for a minute before saying, "There is nothing to tell."

"Well," I replied hesitantly, "what were you doing in that bank?"

"I don't really know," he said quickly and softly.

"Were you going to rob it?" I asked.

That made him angry. "Don't be ridiculous!" Anthony said tersely.

"Do you remember being there?" I probed again.

"Let's just get this over with," Anthony replied, "What can you do for me?"

"Well I know this psychiatrist, Dr. Lewis. He's very good. Maybe he can help." I was worried that would offend him but he actually perked up. "You mean like a temporary insanity thing?" Anthony inquired.

"Well, that's possible," I said, scratching my head and looking at the floor. "I'm sure he could help you if you would be willing to see him." We walked to his sports car where his sons were waiting.

"The number is at the juvenile facility," I told him. We drove there. Anthony's boys stayed in the car. I talked to the outside speaker, went past the security checkpoint and took out my large set of keys to unlock a series of doors that led to my office. As I was flipping for the number, Anthony saw a pair of handcuffs on my desk. "Do you know what it's like to have handcuffs on your wrist?" he said defiantly. I shook my head as I handed him the phone number.

I did not realize as he drove out from the parking lot we had our last face-to-face conversation for many years.

The following week, my secretary at the juvenile facility announced over my intercom, "Two gentlemen are here to see you." I was puzzled. There was nothing on my appointment calendar so I assumed they were salesmen, vendors often came unsolicited.

I invited them into my office and immediately both men produced FBI credentials. "Have a seat," I said. I was not surprised. The FBI visiting is not all that unusual when you work in the criminal justice system.

"We're here to talk about your brothers," one agent said. That afternoon Agent Leroy Himebauch laid out facts too strange to believe. The subsequent trial would make banner headlines and newspaper articles, but I would hear that day that my brothers were the greatest bank burglars in the history of America!

Their crimes began in 1978. Anthony styled hair at The Velvet Brush in Deerfield. My older brother Joseph had rented safe-deposit boxes at the First National Bank of Deerfield and entered several times a week often with a large bag or a small suitcase. He signed a phony name "J. Zito." When they entered the bank vault together, it was usually Joseph who would turn on the charm and talk to the female attendant. They were "casing" the place as Joseph diverted attention. Anthony took an ice pick and punched holes in the alarm system, sound sensors that looked like stereo speakers. On another visit, he placed two alarm clocks in the false ceiling. The clock alarms were set to ring after banking hours.

Early one evening Anthony sat in his car watching the bank. It was past the time the clocks had rung and he watched to see if the police were coming. No one came and he knew the vault alarm had been disabled.

It was a bright Sunday afternoon July 22, 1979. Anthony crept into bushes behind the Deerfield bank and removed a ventilation grate. There was a small conference room just outside the safety deposit vault, where he dropped in. He brought with him food, a drill, four crowbars, two flashlights, two headlamps, two sledgehammers, three chisels, eight screwdrivers, a vise grip, a hacksaw, goggles and a torch. Since there were two sets of flashlights, headlamps and sledgehammers, it was logical that Joseph would join him later, after preliminary work on a concrete wall.

Unexpectedly, a janitor stopped by the bank. He heard a noise in the basement and he was shocked to find Anthony standing on a chair on a table, drilling into a wall. Everywhere was concrete and plaster.

He bluffed the janitor. "Who's going to clean up this mess!?" he demanded.

The janitor said, "I will."
He promptly went to get a broom and other cleaning instruments, thinking that Anthony was a repairman. Minutes later the janitor came back, finding an unfinished hole and tools, but Anthony had departed quickly.

Why the bank of Deerfield? It shared a parking area with another structure, a beauty shop owned by Anthony. He was literally living in his beauty shop and planning the robbery of the very bank where he had an account. It was two days later at the Fourth of July party where he was wearing a cast. He had said it was a tennis accident, but in reality it was from swinging the large sledgehammer against the wall. U. S. Attorney William Colson later referred to Anthony as a "coolheaded man with nerves of steel."

On Friday, April 9, 1981, I was summoned to see Chief Judge Bruce Fawell of the 18th Judicial Circuit Court. He was a stickler for details and if any probation officer failed to investigate properly, he would pounce on them verbally. If someone insulted his presence in the court by not wearing a tie, he would give them a $50 fine, and if they talked back, he would let them stew overnight in the county jail.

There were twenty-six judges in this circuit, and as the chief judge, he wielded immense power. I was understandably nervous. Walking across the parking lot, I wondered if I had failed to do my homework on one of my cases. I went into his large office in the old courthouse building, and sat on the other side of an immense mahogany desk. He hit his fist hard on the desk, catching me off guard spouting, "You are the best damn probation officer I've ever seen!"

Reacting to his fist strike, I did not hear the compliment. The purpose of the meeting was a promotion. I was going to be the next Assistant Warden of a juvenile facility. I had gotten the attention of the "big man" and after working in small offices in both the juvenile and adult divisions of probation, my career was starting to blossom. I felt several feet above the ground as I walked back to my office. This had been a good day, indeed. It was exactly 1:30 p.m. on a Friday.

Twenty-four hours later on Saturday morning I was with my son at a small zoo, Cosley Children's Farm. And fifteen miles north of the court building was the Bank of Barrington, in Barrington, Illinois. With the regular vault attendant on vacation, my brother Anthony used a credit card to open a glass door that led to the vault. He crawled on top of the safety deposit boxes and dropped into a corner. It was a 24-inch square open space. The bank employees did not know of the dead space in the corner. He knew the architectural drawings of the bank that showed the dead space. The thick metal vault door closed at 1 p.m. (on Saturday). It was time-locked and would not open until 7:30 a.m. the following Monday. Ten minutes later an alarm went off and Barrington Police arrived to check the bank. Nothing suspicious was found. They were convinced it was a malfunction. Anthony realized one of the sound sensors was still operational. He crawled out a second time and punctured it. Again an alarm went off and the police arrived. This time they were convinced it was a malfunction so considered the bank safe.

Anthony had a large possession of burglary tools that he had put in a false ceiling during the many times he and Joseph had visited the safety deposit boxes. He had also placed some of the tools in the large box they had rented. It included four flashlights, a sledgehammer, a crowbar, several screwdrivers, tape, batteries, and other instruments. He would breath slowly so as not to consume all the oxygen in the large vault. He worked through the day and through the night punching out locks, cutting through hinges, removing the contents of each vault.

The next morning my family and I attended church at Bethel Presbyterian in Wheaten. As an Elder, I sat with Pastor Bob Harvey and participated in the commemoration of the Lord's Supper. It was Palm Sunday and the beginning of Holy Week, a day churches commemorated the triumphant entry of Jesus into Jerusalem.

Joseph was attending Mass in Melrose Park, but his thoughts were riveted on the bank vault. If Anthony was successful, he would soon be very wealthy. He walked to his car holding a symbolic palm, representative of the palms waved and laid at the feet of Jesus as he entered the city.

As Anthony opened each box, he looked into the lives of strangers. Only the most precious valuables are put into safety deposit boxes...heirlooms, jewelry handed down from parents and grandparents, and hidden treasures, like cash from drug deals and money undeclared to the IRS. In reality, the security boxes of this bank in a town of multi-million dollar homes contained great riches.

I had a relaxing Sunday afternoon with my wife and four-year-old son Luke. I was thirty-five years old and Anthony was forty-one. I had a meager income in the justice system, and Anthony had just become a multi-millionaire. In one box there was a 10-carat diamond ring worth $128,000. In another box, gold coins worth $33,500. Another box contained a platinum and emerald ring worth $15,270. A treasured family brooch worth $10,000 was next snatched. Anthony wasn't interested in paper, documents or securities. He was taking cash, gold coins and jewelry. By Sunday afternoon, he had over two million dollars. His two duffel bags were so heavy, he had to remove silverware and put them back in boxes, although he could not remember the boxes they came from.

Monday morning I was having breakfast as our son was quietly playing with a toy dinosaur. I had just put on my tie, kissed my wife goodbye and drove to the juvenile facility for an 8 a.m. meeting.

Several miles away Joseph sat anxiously in a rented van in the bank parking lot waiting for the appearance of Anthony. The steel locks retracted on the heavy door at 7:30 a.m. The massive door was pushed open by a bank employee. Anthony had swept up the mess and stored it in the false ceiling only hours before. All the security locks had been replaced and everything looked untouched. The vault appeared normal. Anthony was hiding in the corner when the door was opened. Since no employee was waiting outside the vault, he calmly walked out. A bank worker saw Anthony dressed as a construction worker with two large duffel bags as he headed across the parking lot, figuring he was a workman. He went back for a second set of bags.

He and Joseph drove off celebrating their acquired wealth. The crime was still undiscovered. It was thirty minutes later that an employee put a key into a cylinder lock to open a customer's box. The lock fell into the unopened box. The customer did not understand. The employee quickly asked the customer to return to the waiting area. The police and FBI were called and cars came racing in. An FBI agent looked closely at the box and then pushed in the lock of another box. It fell in, too. One by one the FBI discovered 74 safety deposit boxes were missing all their valuables. It was the most successful looting of a safety deposit vault in United States history!

Several months later in December, the largest armed robbery in history would take place at a New York airport. It was mob connected and the subject of a Martin Scorcese film *Goodfellows*, a theft of almost ten million dollars. But my brother's crime was not robbery but burglary, well planned and executed.

The FBI realized they would never know the full extent of the burglary of the First National Bank of Barrington, "easily over three million dollars," Agent Himebauch related to me.

I continued to see my brothers for the next year and a half. They seemed prosperous, yet there was no connection between the attempted burglary of the Bank of Deerfield and the burglary of the Bank of Barrington, at least in terms of a suspect. It was an unsolved crime, nearly perfect.

Anthony and Joseph had meticulously planned the crime. Planning included what to do with the stolen property, referred to as *swag*, the stolen goods that thieves have to liquidate. For that phase they needed to go to a *fence*. And at the level of these gems, they needed a mob network. They pulled emeralds, rubies and diamonds from their settings and throughout the year traded them for cash.

Thus the trip to Geneva, Switzerland, where much of the cash was put in a Swiss bank account, not to be found or traced.

There was a rumor that a tall guy from Chicago in his late forties was fencing gems in New York City; his nickname was "Blue Eyes." Was this my brother Joseph? He was six foot four, had connections in New York (having been raised there), and like my brother Anthony, had blue eyes.

Joseph seemed nervous that year. He was the more emotional of my two brothers, cunning but hotheaded. A few years before, he had organized a 60th birthday party for my mother. It was at a restaurant known to be frequented by and owned by the mob, The Homestead. My mother would say, "The meat is good there because you know where it comes from (*carne buona*)." I had bought my mother a present, but Joseph made it clear to me in the restaurant lobby that I owed him $160 for my share of a large, if not gaudy, gold medallion. The gems on the medallion were the birthstones of all her children and grandchildren. After my father's death, Joseph had become the self-appointed *padrone*.

I stood up to him that day. "You didn't tell me about this gift. We already bought one," I replied.

"That don't matter," Joseph said. "Give me $160 for your share."

"We did not discuss this, " I responded.

"I made the decision!" he blurted back.

Fortunately my mother and the other wives were already seated at the table. Anthony was outside smoking a cigarette.

Then I pushed my brother verbally, "Who made you the boss?" I declared.

He lunged at me and began choking me with his hands. His hands were very tight. At that moment, Anthony rushed in and tried to loosen Joseph's grip. People coming into the restaurant were in shock. Customers moved quickly past us.

Joseph yelled, *"Figlio di puttana*! (Son of a B___!) and other expletives. My face was red and I had marks around my neck. He continued to call me names as Anthony grabbed his arm and said, "Forget it, let's go back to the table!" I went into the restaurant's restroom to compose myself and then returned to the table, my face and eyes red. My wife looked at me bewildered.

Mom asked, "Is everything OK?"

"Fine," I said. But I learned that day that Joseph had the same violent streak of our father. He could not be reasoned with.

His wealth had not changed his temperament. Both acted like ancestors from years past, even acquiring the intense stare of Angelo Genna.

My brothers walked coolly out of the Bank of Barrington with millions of dollars, but they wanted more. They picked another bank in an affluent suburb north of Chicago, the First National Bank of Lake Forest.

Their criminal downfall could best be summed in one word, GREED.

The third bank did not go well. A loose ceiling tile fell and struck a bank customer while in the men's restroom. A janitor saw a foot and within minutes police and FBI agents with guns drawn arrested Anthony. His defeated looking mug shot photo appeared on the front page of the Chicago Tribune newspaper.

Now authorities watched me. My phones were tapped. They examined my bank records. FBI agents came to my office and my home, and I was summoned before a federal grand jury. When I said, "I know nothing about their bank robberies," several jurors laughed. A grand jury member asked, "You have two brothers in crime and a family history of associations and you mean to tell us you're not involved?"

Federal Prosecutor Wilson assured me, "We would never call you to testify against your own brothers." Several months later I received a subpoena for the trial.

"If you refuse to show," the prosecutor said, "we will charge you with contempt of court, punishable by a fine and one year in jail."

Anthony and Joseph were both indicted on seven counts of bank burglary and conspiracy. It was a sad and difficult time for the family and for me. These were not the crimes of past ancestors but my current, immediate family.

Ironically, during the days of the trial I was away from home, in Joilet, lecturing probation officers on ethics and how to give concise court testimony.

The night before the trial, in my small hotel room, I called my wife Regina about midnight. "I don't think I can do this," I told her. "It's just asking too much to testify against my own brothers."

"Whatever you think is best, I'm behind you," Regina responded. And so, I decided not to testify. I turned off the lamp, put my head on the pillow and tried to sleep. I was startled thirty minutes later by the phone ringing. It was not my wife but the federal prosecutor.

"Sorry to call so late," Mr. Wilson said, well after midnight, "but I'm concerned about the weather tomorrow so I'm sending someone to pick you up."

Early the next morning I looked out the window and saw a white car with black walls. Another was parked in the rear.

In all, four FBI agents had come to "escort" me to the federal courthouse.

I was considered a "hostile witness," not present voluntarily but coerced, under threat of punishment, and not fully cooperative. As I sat in the witness box I looked at my brother Anthony sitting behind the defense table. He looked pale and sullen, his eyes downcast (Joseph was in too poor health to stand trial). I saw my mother and other relatives sitting behind him. The prosecutor leafed through pages of legal pad notes as I scanned two eight foot exhibit tables containing gloves, sledge hammers and other burglary tools my brother used.

There was really only one substantial question the prosecutor asked me after I took the oath "to tell the truth, the whole truth and nothing but the truth, so help me God."

"Did either of your brothers ever offer you a large sum of money?" he asked.

I was cut off

I was cut off.

I was cut off from family events and get togethers.

Anthony was convicted in a federal court on April 24, 1985, and received a 20-year prison sentence (Anthony's time in state prison began in 1981). He was taking the heat for Joseph.

The first Christmas after the trial, I received a large box from Anthony. There was no note. It contained every Christmas present we had ever given them.

The largest Chicago newspaper, *The Chicago Tribune* (the same paper that featured headlines about Capone) had his

photo and the headline *Bank Job a Perfect Crime—Almost.*
There was a series of articles, and over the next few months
the story would be reprinted in crime magazines, including
Detective Magazine and in the *Safe Deposit Operations Manual*
by a nationwide organization that trains bank officers.

As I completed this manuscript, a production company
dramatized my brother's crimes. The story appeared on
Court TV in the U. S. and on the show **Masterminds** in
Canada on December 23, 2003, titled "The Perfect Score."

Federal Judge Marvin Aspen said to Anthony, "You are a
very bright and multi-faceted person." He gave Anthony a
$25,000 fine, a 20-year sentence and five years of probation.
Then he added, "I will consider a sentence reduction if
people's property is returned." Anthony insisted he was
innocent and had no idea where any stolen possessions
would be. Aspen also gave him 500 hours of community
service, which included helping bankers make their safety
deposit box areas more secure.

Anthony went immediately to the Metropolitan Federal
Corrections Center in Chicago from the courthouse, a
prison where I had brought many of my Wheaton College
students for evangelism. Next he was transferred to Milan
Federal Prison in Michigan.

My letters were returned unopened, and all my attempts to
contact him were fruitless. Anthony even rebuffed a
chaplain friend I sent to minister to him. "He's the most
hardened person I've ever met," said Chaplain David
Spong, telling me Anthony had "no interest in God
whatsoever."

At this time my son Luke was nine years old and required a
third open-heart surgery. It was a very difficult surgery
because they had to cut through the previous scar tissue
from the past surgeries. Doctors were going to replace a
valve. After some 10 hours a surgical nurse came out to
speak with my wife and me. "We have good news and bad

news," she said, "The surgery was successful, but we are unable to get his heart started."

During open-heart surgery, the heart is literally stopped, bypassed while operated on, and then must be restarted. It was the longest 15 minutes of my life. As my wife and I looked at the clock, we realized we were powerless to do anything. It was an agonizing time. We cried out to God to save our son's life.

Then the nurse returned after 15 minutes and said, "It started." We knew that God had touched our son's body, and as before, we entered the ICU where Luke was buried within a mass of tubes and wires, a drainage tube for blood, thick stitches on his chest, a breathing tube down his throat, an arterial line, a catheter and IVs flowing with antibiotics, fluids and fresh blood. That morning twelve people from our church came before sunrise to donate blood. It was such a meaningful gesture.

Our pastor, Bob Harvey, would make 100 mile round trips daily and just sit in a corner and be with us, a true ministry of presence. Many church friends, including Luke's grade school teacher, came to visit. She posted on his door a sign-up sheet where all his classmates were taking turns in increments of 15 minutes praying for him. I learned you can really experience love and family from people not even blood related.

Because I was cut off from the family, so was our son. It was in many ways the real indication of the Sicilian stubbornness my father demonstrated, an unforgiveness and a resistance to any form of reconciliation.

None of my family except my mother came to visit our son while he was in ICU or during the long recovery process. Joseph dropped off my mother but always remained in his auto parked in front of the hospital. Joseph's anger ran deep. Even from his prison cell Anthony, *the godfather*, controlled Joseph and the others.

Years went by and Anthony insisted that he knew nothing about the burglary at the Barrington Bank. The prosecutors worked out a deal to reduce Anthony's sentence to seven years upon the return of people's valuables.

Although he had steadfastly maintained his innocence, his former wife dropped off a package containing 400 pieces of jewelry at the office of Anthony's lawyer, James Meltreger, on North Avenue in Chicago.

The package included rings and brooches with their stones and valuable gems removed as well as a ring that had contained a 10-carat diamond. Some of the jewelry was counterfeit. The prosecutors were enraged. The judge likewise felt Anthony was trying to "pull a fast one." The deal was called off. Finally several hundred more pieces of jewelry, including gold coins showed up.

According to my mother, "The real thief felt sorry for your brother and turned them in." Mom was easily duped by them. She worked hard at denial, believing their fantasy explanations.

Some of the larger valuables, including a nine-carat diamond were finally returned. The loot had been returned, but not all. The jewelry, according to the FBI, "had evidence it had been water-logged." I remember construction at Joseph's lake house. Joseph was converting his wooden pier to a sturdier concrete pier with cement footings in the summer of 1981. Had it been hidden in one of the concrete piers of Joseph's summerhouse? Anthony continued to serve his eight-year federal sentence following his three years in an Illinois prison.

During that time (1987) Joseph's wife, Marie, who had never worked a day in her life, bought a multi-million dollar restaurant on North Avenue, not far from Tony Accardo's house.

My mother was a frequent entertainer at the restaurant, playing the piano and singing. I asked my mother, "How did Marie get the money to buy such a large restaurant?"

"She saved," was her answer, not wanting to go any further.

While Anthony was in prison, Joseph became very ill and was rushed to a hospital. I received word that some of his organs were shutting down, his kidneys and his liver in particular. He had heart trouble, too. My wife Regina said, "We must go to the hospital and visit him."

My first reaction was, "No."

After the grand jury subpoena, there was a family funeral. I approached Joseph with an extended hand and he turned his back on me and walked away. This was the beginning of the period of being publicly shunned.

Decision Magazine, the magazine of the Billy Graham Evangelistic Association, printed an article about my refusing the burglary money. This so infuriated Joseph's wife that she stormed in where my wife and mother-in-law worked, literally yelling.

That was not the kind of atmosphere I wanted to enter if I went to the hospital to visit Joseph. Yet my wife said, as she had said many times before, "We must do the right thing." But the right thing in this case was very uncomfortable. I dressed in slow motion.

We arrived at the hospital and the timing was perfect. As the elevator doors opened onto the waiting room, no one was there. Everyone had gone to dinner. Then my nephew came out and was very cordial. He said, "It doesn't look good. My dad's really sick." Joseph was in intensive care. I asked if I could see him and my nephew escorted me into the room.

Joseph was on a ventilator connected to tubes, IVs, and a catheter with little output of urine into the collection bag at the foot of the bed.

I said to my nephew, "I'd like to pray." Then I added, "I'm going to touch him." I did not want him to get the impression that I was making a sudden move to pull out any wires or tubes. My nephew nodded.

I put my hands on Joseph's arm. It had been many years since I had been this close or even touched him physically. I prayed for God's healing out loud and as I completed the prayer, my nephew made the sign of the cross as a practicing Catholic. He hugged me and we left.

The next morning I received a phone call from my nephew. "Uncle, it's a miracle! All of my dad's organs are functioning and he's even sitting up." Then there was a pause and he added, "You healed him!"

"No," I said to him, "It was not me, it was God."

I kept in touch with the hospital nursing staff and my nephew to get daily reports of his recovery. Four days later my nephew said by telephone, "My dad wants to see you." I could not believe my ears. I was deeply touched.

I brought my son Luke with me to Good Samaritan Hospital in Downer's Grove. I was nervous, of course. It had been ten years since we talked. We were running several minutes late. Joseph was sitting in a chair talking on the telephone. Before I entered the room, I heard him say, "My brother Donnie's coming. He's late, but should be here any minute."

As I entered the room, Joseph got up, walked to me and gave me a firm hug. It was the moment I had hoped and prayed for. We sat down, and since he had not seen Luke since he was a small child, Joseph was amazed by his height. Luke was a sophomore in high school and had already drawn and published several comics with his skills as an artist. He showed his drawings to his uncle, who looked pleased. After his release from the hospital, we continued to talk by phone every few weeks.

My brothers shared secrets together, many deep, dark secrets. And what at first had seemed like reconciliation soon turned cold. The renewed relationship lasted only four months.

In one of our last phone conversations Joseph said, "You didn't have to talk to them (meaning the FBI). You should have stuck with us. *Famiglia* (family) is more important than anything." When I heard that, I realized his heart had not changed. I felt like God had given him a second chance. He had nearly died and God had healed him but there was no remorse or real change I could see.

In all, Anthony served eleven years (state and federal time consecutively). Joseph threw a large party for him when he was released in 1993. He had a Machiavellian influence over Joseph, and soon we lapsed back into the "cold war" we had experienced for so many years. Anthony insisted that Joseph could not have a relationship with him and me at the same time. And Joseph made a choice. He attended the party, and stopped talking with me.

Soon there was what appeared to be a split between the two brothers. Apparently Joseph had spent much of the unclaimed loot and although Anthony was able to get his hands on money hidden in a Swiss bank, they did not talk to each other for many years.

Anthony first saw me after eleven years at a family funeral of an uncle. I went to a cemetery service, and Anthony arrived not knowing I would be there. He angrily asked, "What is he doing here?" He got in his sports car and promptly drove away.

It was the first time I saw him in years. He was not the same person I remembered before his incarceration. His face color was now gray. His eyes were lifeless. A slight smirk had replaced his smile. He was "a cunning criminal," the prosecutors and FBI agents had said, but he was also devoid of conscience. It was obvious to me he had no remorse for his crime or the effect that it had on our family. Anthony only truly regretted being caught.

He convinced my mother to sell her house, fully paid for, and then move into the top apartment of a large house he had purchased. She told me her money paid for a new heating and air conditioning system, a new roof, and much more.

Mom said, "I know I've made a mistake. I should have been with you, instead I moved to a place where I feel like a prisoner." She did not like her daughter-in-law. They would go away for weekends and not tell Mom they were gone. As Mom grew older and weak, the flight of stairs was very difficult for her to climb. She would often be out of breath and become dizzy by the time she would reach her apartment.

It was difficult for me to visit Mom. In the beginning we had to wait until Anthony was at work or on a trip. Eventually I decided that I could visit my mother whenever I wanted to. I did not worry about him.

1995 was the year my mother began to reveal deeper secrets. Her health was fragile and she sensed time was running out. She showed me photos, explained who some of the more notorious people were and then gave me documents.

I always thought of my grandfather as a gentle, old Italian man, but in truth, I hardly knew him. All my grandparents were deceased when I was born except for my mother's father, Guglielmo. Mom had been in exile for ten years because my grandfather had put out a contract on my father, which he himself was going to fulfill, for eloping with his underage daughter.

My mother often described that exile as one of the worst times of her life (*"il tempo peggiore della mia vita"*). For a decade she was away from her sister, brother, and her parents. Although she saved money to make trips to see her family, my father Matteo would find the money and lose it gambling. His favorite racetracks included the New York tracks of Belmont, Aqueduct, Yonkers and Meadowlands in New Jersey. Mom described how my father would play backroom craps, bet on points in an athletic game, and play poker for hours with high stakes.

And of course, there was the gun; the small black revolver that would come out of the small metal box with the rusty hinges. That familiar creaking sound meant that he had been drinking or was angry. Mom would quickly change the subject, not wanting to talk about the gun. I feared his gun and saw it on more than one occasion; especially the time he pointed it at Mom and myself.

Mom answered a mystery about my grandfather one day. When she returned to Chicago, he departed. If he had missed his daughter so much, why in 1947, did he suddenly leave town? His departure was rapid and it exactly coincided with the death of Al Capone. Did he fear that he had lost the protection of someone he was involved with?

My mother went into detail about his association with the *Terrible Gennas* and his role in producing illegal alcohol for the Capone gang.

After all these years and at age eighty, Mom had no more fears about the truth, no one to protect or cover for, except my brothers. She never told me to keep the secrets to myself.

Mom loved her father, of course, but it did not keep her from revealing his secrets either. "While my mother was dying," she said, "he was with another woman (*con un'altra donna*)." I was startled. From photos I thought they were a close couple. "He was in the movie theater, kissing and hugging this other woman. People saw him. It was a great embarrassment to all of us."

I was born one year after my grandmother Santa's death, and by age one, my grandfather left the large building he had built in the old neighborhood and relocated to a place he had never even visited, Southern California. He bought a 35-acre ranch and lived most of the rest of his life there, in a self imposed exile.

Growing up I rarely saw him except every three or four years. Each time he had a new woman on his arm. My mother informed me it was a new wife. In all, he married five times. She lamented that much of his jewelry and her mother's jewelry was given to each of these women.

He spoke very little English and only near the end of his life came back to Chicago where my mother and her sister Josephine took turns caring for him. We could not really converse. Whenever he left the house, he was eager to show neighbors his diamond stickpin and his rings, which upset my mother.

It must have been difficult for my mother to share those memories with me. We all want our parents to be remembered well. But now, some of the questions were answered. How did an immigrant with no money and no possessions acquire the wealth to buy fine clothes, jewelry, new cars, the first radio, build a barber shop and a large apartment building with three flats and a basement for entertaining? Did all this come from haircuts and shaves? She told me how he produced illegal alcohol for the Genna brothers.

My mother often talked about the old neighborhood. It originated in the Blue Island section of Chicago near Taylor Street, and then moved to Austin Avenue where my grandfather built his building. I was born in that building.

Who were the neighbors? I realize that while many of them were blood related, all were *paisano*, from the same region in Sicily. I was startled when I saw a photograph of what I thought was my grandfather's apartment. The building was identical in every respect; only it was several blocks away on the same street. It was Ralph Capone's building, the brother of Al Capone. My grandfather had the only other building identical to his. There were others on the block as well, including notorious gangsters.

After my brother's release from prison, I began visiting my mother frequently. I simply did not discuss my brothers and that pleased her. I'm not sure to this day what made her start revealing secrets to me. Perhaps it was trust or just a need to tell someone, but I also believe she wanted me to tell her story. It began slowly at first by looking at photos in albums. It must have been difficult for Mom to tell me about her father's infidelities.

We talked about my father's dark side, which I had experienced first hand. Only when she started revealing the identity of "uncles" did I realized our intimate connection to a broader crime family.

A Chicago film magazine was doing an article on one of my films and a writer named Jay Robert Nash was assigned to interview me. We were sitting in the Black Hawk Restaurant in Chicago and as part of the biographical sketch he was asking me about my Chicago upbringing. When I began to tell him about some of the family "connections," he began to quiz me.

"Do you know who I am?" he asked.

I was not sure. Then he pulled out a very large book from a briefcase, **Of Badmen and Blood Letters**. I was familiar with the book. I had forgotten his name. Here was the foremost writer about the mafia in America, the writer of many books. This was an opportunity to verify things my mother had told me. I gave him details about the St. Valentine's Day massacre.

He said, "You are exactly right. But the police do not know the details you just gave me."

I told him of my mother's observations of the Genna brothers, Capone and the people who came to our house. I soon learned from Nash that Mom spoke with crystal clarity about the things she saw and heard during her long life. The luncheon actually gave me a chill, knowing the secrets revealed were reality and not exaggerations.

Mom finally told me the story of the fight between Anthony and my Dad and how Anthony had pinned him to the floor just weeks before he died from a fatal heart attack.

And there were more secrets to come. She talked of the lady in the cemetery that I often saw, the sister of the Gennas, who after all these years still could not understand why anyone would kill her brothers.

Mom told me about my own godfather, how races had been fixed and how his own children went to prison for ghost payrolling in Chicago. "*Vergogna*! (What a shame!)" she would say frequently.

The last time I brought her to the cemetery, Mom was eighty-two. I held her arm tightly because her steps were hesitant and unsure, yet she would glow as she would spot a familiar name and begin to tell stories. I drove my car to a large mausoleum that had the name Giancana etched in stone. "Oh, yes," she said. "He was frying sausages and green peppers."

I did not understand. "What do you mean?" I asked.

"You know, at his place in Oak Park, he was grilling Italian sausage and green peppers, and they killed him," as Mom rested on the concrete bench beside his tomb.

"Who?" I asked.

"Well," she said, "not strangers." She looked off at the horizon as if imaging a scene. "It was a friend ("Amico"), someone he knew. He let him in."

I was still confused. Then she looked at me intently as if trying to teach a lesson. "He knew too much and they had to quiet him," she said in a hushed voice, "*Capire*? (Understand?)"

I knew the name, of course. Giancana had become the *capo di capo* (boss of bosses) in the mid-1950s when Tony Accardo turned over the Chicago mob to him. She gestured the sign of the cross to say a short prayer for his soul.

As we started to drive to a new cemetery location she murmured, "You knew him."

I pressed the brake, startled. "I knew him?"

"When you were a child...the man who played cards with your father...Momo."

Suddenly I realized Mom was talking about someone she had known. "Grandpa knew him. He was young then and kind of wild but a good driver." (By that, she meant a driver for Capone and other gang members.)

"Remember?" she said. "He gave you a finn (five dollar bill) every time."

"Oh," was all I could say as my mind reverted to myself as a boy bartender. He was the man I served bourbon to "straight, no rocks (ice)."

In her heart, Mom knew the crimes Anthony and Joseph had committed but could not bear to face the truth. A mother loves her children no matter what they do or become. When she would ask Anthony and Joseph if the family would ever have unity, Anthony would say, "Give it time."

But there was not enough time for mother. She was rushed to a hospital early one Saturday morning in 1997. She was about to be wheeled in for a heart operation. She was eighty-three, weak and frail, hardly a good candidate for major surgery. Mom already had a breathing tube and was not able to talk to me. She grabbed my hand and squeezed it and I could see that she desperately wanted to say something. It was so awkward being in the hospital room with my brothers. By now they had effectively poisoned their own sons (my nephews). One of Anthony's sons was especially discourteous. Opened doors nearly slammed into my face and they gave a look of resentment toward my very presence.

Mom came out of the surgery alive but in a coma. She had a stroke during the surgery and all I could think of was that she would be in a vegetative state in a nursing home the rest of her life. That was hardly the way my mother would have wanted to end her life. She was an accomplished pianist and singer, and paralysis would have been a living hell for her.

My brother Anthony told the hospital staff that he had *Power of Attorney*. He was lying. One day a priest informed me of some decisions Anthony was making. I responded by asking the priest, "Have you seen the proof of the Power of Attorney? We, her sons, share it equally." His deceit was now discovered and Anthony and Joseph were forced to talk with me. In a hallway one afternoon there was a sterile, emotionless conversation.

"We've got to do what's best for Mom," Joseph said without eye contact. "If she's not going to get better, we need to pull the plug," Anthony added, also not looking at me.

I told them I would "think about it." In the meantime, Mom lay in bed with a spasm in her neck, eyes closed, oblivious to the world.

Joseph was convinced she would get better. He would often say to her, "Hang on, hang on, you are going to get better, just fight this." Several days after the surgery, I found myself alone in the room with my mother. All had gone to dinner. It was then that I leaned close to her ear and said, "Mom, trust Jesus, trust Jesus." Then I added, "It's okay to leave. It's okay to go home." Suddenly her head turned in my direction and her eyes opened. Mom appeared to be looking right at me. Her eyes filled with tears. Again, I repeated, "Trust Jesus. Take His hand and go home." As I squeezed her hand, her eyelids slowly closed.

I do not know if she heard me that late afternoon. I do not know if that was a spontaneous reaction or she understood. But I like to believe she did.

The next day my wife returned from work and said, "Let's go visit your mom at the hospital."

The hospital was very far from our home. "I'm really tired," I said. "Let's go tomorrow morning."

But my wife had an instinct, and I'm sure now it was God's leading. "I think we should go now," she said.

I really was not in the mood but did it to please her. As we were walking toward the ICU, a nurse who had been very kind to us came rushing toward us. "I'm so glad you got here. Your mother's dying and your brother told us he called you." Of course, he had not called us. He had lied to the nursing staff as usual, and they thought we simply were taking our time. Joseph knew but chose not to come.

It was all very strange. The setting was not how a screenwriter would develop a story. Anthony and his new wife, a much younger woman I had never been introduced to, were on one side of the bed and my wife and I on the other. I held my mother's hand. She had been weaned off food, IVs, and her breathing tube, and I watched the color in her face slowly vanish. Her eyes darkened. Then I heard one last sigh. I looked up at the monitor and I saw the flat line indicating her heart had stopped beating, after eighty-three years.

I half expected at a time like that, my brother would say something to me, but true to form, he was totally quiet. He turned and with his wife walked quietly out of the room. It was a sad time for me. The nurse gave my wife and me some time alone.

Mom always had beautiful blue eyes, and as my grandfather would say, "*Rosa e´ una cimba dagli occhi azzurri.* (Rosa the girl with the blue eyes.)" I gently lifted one eyelid to see her eye one more time. I could only imagine what those eyes had seen from the turbulent years of the Gennas and the Capones to the many parties and Italian feasts.

I asked the nurse to remove her wedding ring, which she always wore, long after my father's death. I held it in my hand. Suddenly, Anthony stormed into the room and over my mother's warm body bellowed, "Where's the ring?!" Without so much of a word, I handed it to him. He then took it and left the room abruptly.

Fred Cappetta had been the funeral director for our family and relatives for over fifty years. He handled the arrangements for my father in 1969. Although he had long since retired and was in his late 70s, out of friendship for my mother he was going to take care of the arrangements.

The next morning we went to the funeral home. Being the youngest (although fifty-one at the time), my brothers talked to the funeral director as if I was not in the room. And, in the case of Joseph, the money flowed to chase his guilt. He asked for thousands of dollars worth of roses to be spread over the coffin. He and Anthony reserved the largest parlor room. Then it was time to pick a casket, and of course, Joseph did most of the talking. He continued to upgrade and the casket he chose, although pretty, was extremely expensive. My mother had beautiful party dresses when she went dancing. As we had discussed the subject, I instinctively knew that she would want to be viewed in one of those dresses. Soon a verbal argument broke out and Anthony insisted that it would be a closed casket. Joseph said, "Let's wait and see." The older relatives coming always expected to view the body as a traditional part of the visitation and my mother would have wanted to be in one of her beautiful dresses. Her new daughter-in-law however brought a leopard print mock turtleneck. It was bunched in a box, wrinkled and disheveled.

I loved my mother and my mother loved me, so all of this seemed unimportant. Then Joseph started talking about a vault. "I want the best vault. The kind with the tongue and groove that is hermetically sealed." Of course one of the funeral directors was also a salesman and was happy to oblige. But at one point, Joseph said, "I want to be able to open this casket in 100 years and have her look as good then as she looks today." Another funeral director gave me a look and I whispered under my breath, "We are not going to be here in 100 years." Between the two brothers they ordered black limousines that would be empty and reserved the largest parlor that would never be a quarter filled.

The funeral director did a fine job and my mother's body looked very presentable. Joseph arrived and agreed that her face looked good. Anthony arrived and said, "I want this lid closed!" Suddenly a verbal fight broke out with incredible expletives. Then they began shoving each other, almost knocking Mom's casket off the platform. Some of the older relatives, my mother's cousins, were mortified.

Later that evening about 8 p.m., Anthony was standing in front of the funeral home smoking a large cigar. I went outside and stood next to him. He knew I was there but did not look at me. I felt compelled to say something. "You're my brother. I don't care what you think of me. I love you, and I always will love you." There was a long difficult silence. Suddenly he turned his head toward me. I could see his face lit by the light of the blue neon funeral home sign. He gently blew cigar smoke in my direction saying, "I don't hate you. (He paused) ... You just don't exist." Then he turned and slowly walked away. I stood there chilled by the cold air. That was our last conversation.

Although I had thought the grudges would have ended when my father died, Anthony had followed so well in Dad's footsteps. It was truly a generational curse. I was now on his black list. I was a non-person. I was cut off.

For the next two days there were very few people who came since many friends of Mom's and relatives were deceased. Those who came essentially came to private funerals. Joseph stood on one side of the cavernous room, Anthony in another, and myself in still another section. Each of the brother's friends was not introduced to the others. There was no receiving line. No more than thirty people ever filled the huge room.

Respecting my mother's wishes, she was brought to a Catholic church, the one that I was raised in, St. Gertrude's. The priest understood that after his message and prayers, I would read the 23rd Psalm (her favorite), and then the church service would conclude.

On this day it was apparent that Joseph and Anthony were no longer talking, and during the service the priest asked the congregation to turn and with a handshake express the "Peace of Christ." Joseph extended his hand to Anthony who turned around and used several extreme expletives. The older relatives were again shocked. My wife began to cry because their behavior was so crude. She turned to me and whispered, "Your mom deserves better."

I went to the pulpit and read the 23rd Psalm as planned. And then as the priest got ready to end the service, Anthony suddenly got up and started walking toward the pulpit. He was swinging an umbrella. The priest looked at me as if to say, "What's happening?" I knew what the umbrella was about. It had a steel tip and this was going to be used as a weapon if anyone tried to stop him. He went up to the pulpit and explained how "no one really knew my mother as I did." Then he pointed in my direction and said,

"She never loved you." That didn't make me feel bad since I knew it was not true, but it was so disrespectful. As he stepped down from the pulpit, he gave his two sons a *high five* as if to say, "I showed them."

Joseph was so infuriated that after the service in the small cemetery chapel, he drove off and did not come to the luncheon for the relatives.

I waited until Mom's casket was put into the vault, and then gently kissed the lid and put a rose on it. I was glad she was finally at peace. As my wife and I walked out of the small funeral chapel, Mr. Cappetta, the funeral director who worked professionally for well over 50 years, said, "You know, I have seen many things during my years as a funeral director. I have seen families who don't get along and people who quarrel, but in all my years I have never seen a worse family than yours!"

My mother's wishes had been to divide her savings into three equal shares, but of course, that is not what my brothers wanted. They claimed they found a "new will" written in my mother's handwriting. It had no date and was not notarized. I had an attorney call them but Anthony became so infuriated he left a threatening message on my phone machine. I decided money was not worth it. I let them do as they pleased. But they had not read the will (which I easily recognized as her handwriting) with any detail. My wife was left a ring that had belonged to Texas Guinan, a mobster's girlfriend, movie star and performer who ran a speakeasy for the mob in New York. On one of his pawnshop visits, my father had acquired her famous ring. My mother, who always loved my wife Regina, left her the ring. I promptly received a phone call from Joseph. "I want that ring!" he said, "I'm giving it to my granddaughter." I told him that we were going to abide by the terms of the will they had accepted. He cursed and slammed the phone.

According to the will, my wife also received the gold medallion, my mother's 60th birthday gift. After my brother

Joseph choked me in the restaurant lobby, he removed my birthstone from the medallion. Now it was coming to us.

One cold evening I was standing outside of the door to my brother Anthony's house to pick up the medallion. She wore it for twenty-three years without my stone. I rang the doorbell. After some 30 seconds a light came on, and he opened the door. He tossed the brooch to me and then as I began to speak, slammed the door in my face. He barely missed my nose. That was the last time I ever saw Anthony.

Some time later I accepted a position to be president of a large ministry in Texas and while moving called Joseph. He answered the phone with a friendly voice. When I said, "This is your brother Don," there was a silence.

"I thought maybe we could get together for coffee," I said.

"I'm busy," he said, snarling.

"Well, it could be any time," I responded.

"I'm busy!" he said again.

"Well, I just thought I would tell you I'm moving. In fact, there's a moving truck in my driveway." Again there was silence.

"Don't you even want to know where I'm going?" I asked.

"I don't care!" he responded and hung up the phone abruptly. And that was the last time I ever heard my brother Joseph's voice.

For a brief time when he apparently thought he was going to get the ring, we talked. But with Joseph it was always *"how can you prove your loyalty."* He had asked so many times in the past, "Can you talk to a judge you know about a family situation?" He wanted influence. In divorce court, he hoped for a favorable ruling for his son. In criminal court, he sought to get a reduced sentence for a drug-abusing nephew.

Joseph was a devout Roman Catholic, but his confessions appeared surface because he never could forgive or ask for forgiveness. To my brothers I had "gone bad (*e' andato a male*)." I had violated *omerta*. I talked about the family. I had talked about the family to strangers and with the law.

My mother loved all of her children but had to exercise incredible denial about my older brother's behaviors.

There are musical notes etched in my mother's cemetery headstone. The sight of that would have made her happy.

Anyone who knew my mother knew music was an intrinsic part of her life. It brought her joy in difficult times, and she brought joy to thousands by sharing her gift.
My mother was a *flapper*. As a young girl she wore the typical tight dress and fashioned her hair with "spit curls" using an iron. She danced to the music of the *Roaring Twenties* and the early thirties: the Black Bottom, the Charleston, and the Lindy Hop. My parents would go ballroom dancing and dance the Tango, the Foxtrot, the Waltz and the Cha-Cha during the late 1940s and 1950s. She often lived for Saturday nights to escape from her exile in New York's tenements to dance to a live orchestra and listen to the top crooners of the era, like Russ Columbo. My father brought my mother to a New Year's Eve party at a hotel ballroom in Manhattan and she described the music of Guy Lombardo and his orchestra, The Royal Canadians.

I enjoyed listening to my mother's stories about the ballrooms. She would have a twinkle in her eyes, and I could tell she was seeing those days in her memories. I would hear the slang from my mother's era called "Jive Talk." From the Roaring Twenties came terms of endearment like "Baby" and "Doll," which my father said to my mother when courting.

Both Chicago and New York referred to the 1920s as the *Roaring Twenties*. I assume my mother and father went to "speak-easys," a place where you had to know a password, to gamble and consume illegal alcohol. For fifty cents, my father's family in New York could go to Radio City Music Hall and see the Ziegfield Follies. When officials began to renovate the grand old movie theaters, mostly built in the 1920s, I could understand why the drive-in was such a poor substitute. Mom would say, "It was like being in a church. Sometimes we accidentally knelt down (genuflected) because although the statues were of Greek and Roman gods without looking closely they would seem like statues of the saints in neighborhood churches." These theaters had real pipe organs that elevated from the floor. They also had live stage shows before the movies. At the Paramont in New York, singers like Frank Sinatra in the 1940s would perform before the showing of a movie. The twenties were a whirl of organized crime and gang battles but also an exciting era of musical performers, grand theaters, dramatic buildings on the New York and Chicago skylines, and the integration of Italian-Americans into the life and culture of the New World. My mother ignored the crime and focused on the music.

There was a great outpouring of sorrow at the death (at age 31) of an Italian movie star and idol from the silent era, Rudolf Valentino (Rudolfo d'Antonguolia). She would say, "He gave us chills. There was something about his look in *The Sheik*. Every girl wanted to marry him." My father witnessed the crowds of fans on the streets of Brooklyn in public mourning when Valentino died, not unlike the response to the death of Elvis years later in Memphis.

In the 1960s my mother began playing professionally in clubs in and around Chicago using the stage name *Rose Carmen*. She kept a box of newspaper clippings, reviews, and photos advertising her engagements. After my father's death, because he left virtually no savings, she had to support herself through her musical performances so she continued to perform not only at clubs and restaurants and also weddings, bar mitzvahs, and family celebrations well into her seventies.

One day I was talking with her on the phone and after we had finished, she walked away believing she had hung up the phone, but the line was still open. I heard her singing as she accompanied herself on the piano. She was performing alone, delighted to be singing the old Italian ballads. There was no audience as she turned eighty. I continued to listen on the phone for nearly twenty minutes. The agility of her fingers was slower. She occasionally hit a wrong note and her voice was thinner and weaker, not the strong voice I remembered growing up when people would say she could "belt out" the songs. I heard her perform hundreds of times at the height of her music career, but I most remember listening to her on the phone that evening as she played, perhaps taking her back to the old neighborhood, to Reese Park, or the parties in my grandfather's basement. Mom played for priests and mobsters, alike.

I was cut off from the family but not from my memories. Many of those memories were good and warm.

When I began talking about my family and the secrets my mother revealed, I wondered why so many other relatives remained silent. Surely they knew many of the facts I had discovered, but I think they remained silent out of a fear of loss. The fear they would be cut off socially and culturally from the family. "Cutting off (*ha tagliato*)" was what Sicilians like my family did. The cost for revealing secrets, the cost of talking with strangers would be that you would no longer be welcome at the parties for first communions and confirmations, the celebrations of weddings, the holidays, or the luncheons after infant baptisms. I understand their fear because I feel the loss of so many of those family events, even today. I also know the cost of compromising one's integrity is much higher. It is better to be able to live with yourself, have inner peace and a clear conscience than be at a family celebration knowing deep inside that you had sold out.

I am blessed

I am blessed.

I am blessed far more than I deserve.

God has given me experiences I could have never imagined as a young boy growing up in our old Italian neighborhood.

When I share my story in juvenile facilities, especially talking about the crimes of my family, I will invariably have a few young people say, "You should have kept the money," or "That was a mistake not staying with family," or "You could have been a boss today."

Movies like *The Godfather*, *The Untouchables*, *Casino*, and *Goodfellows* and TV shows like *The Sopranos* make the mob look human and three dimensional, but they also tend to glamorize their lives.

There is nothing glamorous. The only excitement is an adrenaline rush during a crime; however, there is constant stress, always looking over your back (not just worrying about the police and the FBI) but also taking a hit from your own mob or group.

In this book, I talked about many crime figures, some well known, many who my family knew or were related to, but it is important for me to emphasize that in almost every case, they had a bad ending. Few died of natural causes.

Let me review a few fates:

- **Dion O'Banion** controlled the north side of Chicago but was gunned down in his own flower shop by Capone's men.

- **Frankie Yale** was brought in from New York to kill some of Capone's rivals. The homicide squad of Scalise and Anselmi, however, were sent to New York to kill him.

- **Mayor Anton Cermak**, who stood up against Capone, was assassinated.

- The six **Genna brothers** were all assassinated, three of them in a three-month period.

- Bloody Angelo's father-in-law **Henry Spignolia** was killed on mere speculation, in case he was planning revenge.

- The homicide squad of **John Scalise** and **Alberto Anselmi** were bludgeoned to death by the boss himself, Big Al, during a dinner in their honor.

- My great **Uncle Vito** was executed with a shot to the back of the head.

- **Jack McGurn** had nearly 30 notches on his machine gun until he was shot and killed in a bowling alley.

- **Al Capone** was sentenced to prison, first the Atlanta penitentiary, then Alcatraz where untreated syphilis rotted his brain. In his forties, he no longer knew who he was and would babble incoherently.

- **Jimmy Hoffa** stood up to Robert Kennedy, and served a prison term before President Nixon pardoned him. He intended to regain control of the Teamsters Union when he disappeared. It is rumored that he is encased in cement under a highway.

- **Robert Kennedy**, who took a hard stand against organized crime, was assassinated, as was his brother, **President John Kennedy**.

- **Jack Ruby**, who killed **Lee Harvey Oswa**ld, died in prison of questionable circumstances..

- **Johnny Roselli** said too much about what he knew about Jack Ruby and ended up in an oil drum floating off the coast of Miami.

- **Sam Giancana** took over the Chicago mob for 20 years but was assassinated in his own home "Sicilian style."

- **Carmine Galante** was shot while eating in a restaurant, just like the scene in *The Godfather*.

- **Paul Castellano, Tony Spolotro**, and **Dominick Napolitano** were all shot and killed by the mob, not the police. Being "made men" didn't protect them.

- **John Gotti** died in a federal prison.

- **Joseph Bonanno** controlled the five families of New York but in his old age ended up in a federal prison and died upon release.

- **Matteo Smarto**, my father, lost far more money than he ever won as a compulsive gambler and died relatively young of a heart attack with little savings.

- My grandfather, **Guglielmo Cappitelli**, abruptly left Chicago within weeks of Capone's death. He bought a remote farm in southern California and went on to marry five times, (and divorced each in turn) living alone, away from his family and the old neighborhood for 30 years.

- My brother **Anthony** received a 20-year prison sentence after being arrested in a bank and served 11 years (4 years longer than Capone).

If crime "pays," it is only in the short term. Most of these people were not killed by the police. In fact, more often than not, it was the mob that killed them.

Real life is not like the movies. The more information these people knew, the more of a threat they were and the more likely they were to be a target.

It is not easy to escape such a crime tradition. It is even more difficult to break from a Sicilian family with such strong social and cultural ties. It is also difficult to break the *omerta* that says implicitly never talk about the family with strangers.

I know my mother wanted a better life for me. For years she covered the identity of "uncles" and the associates of my father. Growing up I rarely saw my grandfather with the exception of a few hours every few years as he was passing though town with a new wife. We only made one visit to his California farm. Speaking no English, he never told me about the old days or his activities in Little Italy, but Mom knew it all.

As Mom reached her eighties she revealed secrets. She told me of my grandfather's infidelity, our family's close ties to the *Terrible Genna's*, and how my grandfather acquired most of his money, not through the barbershop but through the production of illegal alcohol.

Even as she told the stories, she still would put them in the best light. She would say, "Sure, Angelo shot people, but they were rivals, people trying to hurt his business." She would also emphasize their good characteristics; how the *Terrible Genna's* were "generous and enjoyed a good party."

Mom talked about the soup kitchens Capone set up in Chicago that served three hot meals a day for the people hard hit by the Depression. She also talked about how the people of Chicago honored him by giving him a standing ovation at the baseball park. Mom regretted that Capone did not have a more lavish funeral like the ones she had seen for other gangsters.

My brothers did not instantaneously become criminals. It was something that naturally evolved. Beating up people in school came natural. Breaking the law as teenagers, drinking and gambling was second nature. They simply followed the "family ways" which led to greater crimes.

Why do I feel blessed?

I have been happily married for nearly thirty years to a wonderful Christian woman God sent into my life. Together we have made a home of peace that honors God. It is a wonderful feeling to work hard and purchase possessions from your own earnings, not acquiring stolen property.

Doctor Idriss, our son's heart surgeon, never believed Luke would live past the age of five, and about that age I would see him sitting in a windowsill watching other small boys playing soccer. He enjoyed drawing and I would encourage him in that pursuit. Several years ago my wife and I attended a one-man show of our son Luke's art, a requirement as a Fine Arts major for his Bachelor of Arts degree. It was a moment of great joy for us as parents. As I watched him cross the stage with cap and gown to receive his college degree, I could only be reminded of the mercies of God. The doctors did not have the last word. A beautifully illustrated comic tract that our ministry Youth Direct has used across America was drawn and created by him.

God has given me gifts that I have been able to use. I have been a keynote speaker at conferences across America, appeared on many radio and television shows and have had my opinion sought by major newspapers. I was quiet and shy as a child, so anyone can blossom.

I once had an English teacher in junior high, Miss Cain, who told me I had "no writing skills" and, as far as she could determine, "no potential." With eight published books, many widely read, it demonstrates some teachers do not have the final word, either.

A guidance counselor in high school advised me that I was "not college material," yet I have had the privilege of teaching at many fine schools, including Trinity University and Wheaton College. I still maintain contact with former students around the country who themselves are doing worthwhile and admirable service with their lives.

How could I not feel blessed? I have had the opportunity to travel around the world and meet many interesting people and see many historic sights.

After the collapse of the Soviet Union, I was the first person to have the privilege of preaching the gospel in the largest prison in Moscow, Buterka Prison, with 6,500 inmates. No one had openly preached Christ for over seventy years. In small dimly lit cells containing 60 inmates, the prisoners would reach out and touch me gently on the arm, the shoulder or the back while I spoke. When I asked what the prisoners were doing, my interpreter said, "To them, you represent God." That was incredibly humbling and every time I share my testimony and the work of grace in my life, I always count it a privilege.

The message of Romans Chapter 3 in the Bible's New Testament is that anyone, no matter where they come from, no matter what kind of family they have or what sins they have done, can be saved from their sins and can have eternal life.

I should be in a very different place today. It would be more logical for me to follow the ways of my family, swallowed by their patterns and crimes. If you are a younger person reading this, imagine for a moment why a simple boy from an Italian ghetto with a family involved in crime has been with so many prominent people. Only the grace of God can explain that.

In ministry I have had the privilege of meeting Bill Bright, Henry Blackaby, Charles Stanley and Billy Graham. In government, I had a meeting with Attorney General Edwin Meese. (He was late for the meeting because he had to attend a meeting of the Security Council at the White House as they were bombing Libya on that day. He returned from the White House to meet with me for an hour.) I also met and had a long meeting with Senator Mark Hatfield and the Chief Justice of the Supreme Court, Warren Burger. (Senator Hatfield endorsed several of my books, and before his retirement was dubbed "The Conscience of the Senate.") Let me emphasize that in meeting with the Attorney General I was meeting with the highest law enforcement officer in the country. In meeting with the Chief Justice, this was the highest judge of the highest court in America. I remember after our 90-minute meeting (which was his last formal appointment during his tenure as Chief Justice) I walked down the granite steps and remembered my humble upbringing and how only God could have arranged such a meeting.

And of course, the meeting I will never forget a 90 minute meeting with President Ronald Reagan. He had just left office, and in addition to a conversation and an interview, he received several of my books, including my autobiography, for his Presidential Library. He was kind and gracious.

I do not recount these facts to boast because the Bible says if we should boast about anything we should boast in the Lord.

Having read my story, I want to demonstrate what a powerful God can do when we make the right choice. I won many awards over the years and have plaques and trophies from documentary films including the New York Independent Film Festival and twelve Angel awards. But the greatest thing is to have your name written in the Book of Life. Some day all the plaques and trophies will be packed away in a box collecting dust. They really mean very little. All accolades are temporary and they all tarnish. The most important goal is our faithfulness to God.

There is no price tag on peace or spiritual life or character. Character cannot be bought and it is more important than fame, which Shakespeare referred to as the "bubble reputation." I have been most blessed because I am a child of God and I know that I have eternal life.

If you, the reader, currently have troubles in your life and if you have a broken or dysfunctional family or friends pulling you into crime, know that you have a choice just as I had a choice. I am not saying it is easy, but you can decide on any day to take a new path and turn away from crime and sin.

Life does not turn out the way we expect. If you live long enough, you will experience many trials, difficulties and pain. But when you turn your life over to God, you have the assurance that He will never leave you and never forsake you.

Even if you are locked in a juvenile institution or a prison, know that God may allow a valley in your life to mold you, get your attention and turn you into the kind of person He wants you to be.

My answer to Carlos' question, "What made you change your ways?" is a simple one, **the power of God**. I was not looking to break away from my family and their criminal traditions, but God became real to me in a way I can only partly explain in words.

If you abandon crime, might it create a division with friends and family? Yes. Jesus himself had family members that criticized him and even called him "crazy," but he made it clear that putting God first is more important than family.

For me, following God was the opposite of the Sicilian Code. It was not an easy step to put God before my family, but it was the right thing to do.

I am blessed.

I am blessed more than I deserve.

And God will bless you, too, if you give your heart to him.

Epilogue

I can trace my family back to 1840 in Sicily. My great grandfathers were barrelmakers in a Marsala winery. They were honest, hard working people. Perhaps the affluence, opportunities, and temptations of America corrupted many in the family, but these were choices they made.

My parents had the last full blooded Sicilian union. My brothers married German and Irish women and my wife is half Italian, from a region in central Italy. I am, therefore, the last first generation, full Sicilian in our family. Time changes tradition and even culture.

When a young person tells me they can't get out of a gang, I tell them "God got me out of one of the biggest gangs in

America, a crime family." Let me review some of my families' history.

One of the earliest stories my mother told me was of Teresa Fiorino, my great aunt who in 1886 was accused of murdering a man. The family bribed police for her escape from Marsala, Sicily.

My grandfather, Guglielmo, left the poverty of Sicily and soon became wealthy, not as a barber (although his clients were wealthy, powerful mobsters) but by producing illegal alcohol for the *Terrible Gennas* and the Capone crime organization.

My father Matteo had a rough upbringing in the overcrowded Italian ghetto of New York. He used his fists in the boxing ring to win matches and that same brute force to collect union dues, deal with *scabs* (those who cross the picket line to work), and to settle union negotiations.

My great uncle Vito was shot in the back of the head mob style, although my mother insisted it was mistaken identity.

I learned about the secret conversations in the basement of my grandfather's building. My father knew and my mother danced with the Sicilian homicide squad of John Scalise and Alberto Anselmi who committed the St. Valentine's Day Massacre.

I was, in every sense of the word, *schooled*. My teachers were my family. When my father was stopped for a speeding ticket, I watched him hand the officer a driver's license with a folded $20 bill. The officer would come back and hand him only the license telling him to be more careful.

I waited in the car, sometimes for hours, while my father placed bets at a local bookie joint. At age eight, I learned to mix drinks and serve them to the men in the back room playing poker. At my godfather's house as a child, I watched as a parade of people come to pay their respects;

an influential Chicago alderman, a police captain, a few "soldiers," and a *capo,* and even the parish priest. Together my father and godfather bet on fixed races.

I was also schooled by my father's demeanor—eruptions of anger and swearing, throwing objects and wildly waving his gun when he was drunk or enraged.

I grew up learning about my father's *enemy list.* People I was taught to respect and love were banished. We were not allowed to see them or talk to them. Under the protection of my mother, there would be the secret trips to visit an aunt, an uncle or a cousin on the list. My mother always insisted, "Don't tell your father." But occasionally when he found out about a secret visit, he would explode. I watched my father and mother scream at each other, break dishes and at other times not talk to each other for weeks.

My mother often talked about her forced marriage and underage elopement by gunpoint with my father and his bodyguard Sammy, a purported loan shark enforcer. It was a source of great sadness for her.

After my father's death, I had hoped for a cessation of the hostility and crime, but after the disappearance of family friend Fritz and the discovery of his brutally dismembered body in an automobile trunk, I began to wonder.

Soon, Joseph and Anthony were engaged in secret rendezvous, meetings and the *"walk and talk".* Then finally came the Easter Sunday when my brothers offered me the $50,000 and told me it was time to join their "business."

My brothers, of course, carried on in Dad's tradition and in many respects were worse. From their perspective, the $50,000 offer was gracious. They were setting me up with a front and I would be part of the family "business." They were providing for my future financially. It had worked for other family members and they must have seen it as a way for the three brothers to work together. They were not merely disappointed but enraged on the day I refused the money.

To my oldest brother Joseph, I was always the "odd one." I was not following in the family footsteps.

To Anthony, I was seen as terribly naïve, not understanding bribery as a way of life, or cutting corners to get ahead.

Both brothers always viewed the system as corrupt and therefore everything from my church attendance to patriotism was simply giving in to sentimentality.

By the time my brother Anthony started calling himself the "godfather" it was no longer a family joke and I realized that he required, if not demanded, homage. Anthony was smarter than my older brother Joseph and always called the shots.

All Joseph really wanted was my respect and obedience. My older brother had taken over the role of "patriarch" or "*padrone* (boss)." When he made a decision, he did not want it questioned, such as the gift for my mother's 60th birthday. I still vividly remember him choking me in the vestibule of the restaurant because I said "no" to him.

Being a pureblooded Sicilian, I was to inherit the Sicilian vendetta, the grudges, my father's expulsion of people and *omerta*, the code of silence in which you never talk about family matters with anyone. And then my brothers hit the headlines, becoming the greatest bank burglars in the history of America.

In her later years my mother began to unravel the secrets. The secret that my father had really made a good salary, but as a gambling addict had heavy losses that resulted in such debt that he even pawned my mother's wedding ring. There were secrets that included extended family members who were contract assassins, who kidnapped and tortured people.

These are ten of the crimes that my family were involved in:

- Illegal gambling
- Possession of stolen property
- Fencing
- Bribery of officials
- Racetrack fixing
- Fraud
- Ghost payrolls
- Burglary
- Battery
- Murder

ILLEGAL GAMBLING My father's use of bookie joints was illegal.

POSSESSION OF STOLEN PROPERTY Often relatives would wear furs or new suits or have a new color TV set that "fell off the back of a truck." It was not always a simple hijacking of a truck or railroad car. There was a mob term, *bust out*, that meant if someone owed you a debt and they owned a business, you would have them use their credit to buy a load of stereos, TV sets, furs, anything that could be sold easily at a reduced price. The guy in debt, of course, could not pay back his creditors but sometimes would take a second mortgage and eventually file bankruptcy. The good part for him was that he did not get his kneecaps broken and the family got to share the goods. Our family possessed many stolen clothes and articles.

FENCING It was not just a question of my brothers stealing gold coins and jewelry from vaults, but of knowing how to change it into usable cash. The *swag* has to be liquidated and my brothers had mob connections that fenced hot goods in Chicago and New York.

BRIBERY OF OFFICIALS There were politicians as well as police that looked the other way. Going back to the Gennas and Capone the family had to grease the palm of officials to keep in business. My grandfather and my father bribed officials.

RACETRACK FIXING The phone tips that my father and godfather received were about jockeys paid to hold back a good horse or a drug given to speed up a horse with high odds. When younger, my father bet on fixed boxing matches, called "taking a dive."

FRAUD Joseph had been involved in many schemes but once had a plea bargain with the state's attorney (who eventually became governor) over coins and commodities that were sold but never delivered. My brother cut a deal as his partner was hiding in Las Vegas to escape conviction.

GHOST PAYROLLS My godfather's family were involved with "ghost payrolling" in Chicago. Paychecks were received for nonexistent work, a tradition that went back years. Many were sent to federal prisons.

BURGLARY My brothers robbed federal banks, *specifically* vaults, holding the distinction of being the *greatest bank burglars* in the history of America, stealing over 3.5 million dollars from several banks.

BATTERY There were many relatives, including my brothers, who used a short bat or club to settle a grievance. Some family members broke kneecaps when payments fell behind. My mother insisted that my father (a former boxer) had beaten a man so severely in Brooklyn that he died of his injures.

MURDER There were many cousins going back to the era of prohibition that committed murder. Did Anthony murder his business partner? Perhaps no one will ever know.

I recount these crimes to answer the initial question, what could have caused me to change? I want to lead you, the reader, to realize that it certainly was not within my power to break away from a Sicilian family tradition and a family involved in crime for over 100 years.

If I have given any reader the impression that it is *fun* to be in a crime family, you have missed my point. Only television and movies make it attractive. There is a certain amount of adventure in committing crimes and an exhilaration of getting away with something, but it does not last. Sicilian mobsters sit with their backs to the wall, because their enemies come from behind, and assassins are often someone they know, approaching them with a smile. It is no way to live, watching your back or knowing that someone who appears as a friend is going to *whack* you.

I was not really looking for God, but God sought me. He pursued me with a free gift we call grace. I cannot explain it. Even today I do not understand it. It does not make any sense why a good God would not just leave me to wallow in the sinful behaviors of my family.

I had many motivations for studying to be a priest. One was simply escape. I wanted to get away from the turmoil of my family and hide from their criminal ways. Another reason was bad theology. I really thought I could "save" my whole family by doing something good with my life.

Everyone must come to God on their own. I thought by being super spiritual, I could get them all into heaven. I was misguided believing if I did enough good works I could overcome the contamination of a crime family with a long history of evil associations. I acted holy and did not realize that I was a sinner in need of grace, just like them. It came as a stark revelation to me that my sins were no better than those of the *Terrible Gennas*, the homicide squad of Scalise and Anselmi, and Capone. My thoughts were impure, my spirit just as rebellious, and my sins just as black as any mobster, in God's view.

If you are any student of history, you have come to the conclusion by now that today I should be a mob boss, or in prison, or dead. It is entirely logical that I should have gone in that direction. Forces of ethnicity, culture and family are so strong that I should not have been able to resist them.

And that is why I can take no credit for anything good I
have done with my life. Compassion for troubled youth,
especially those in trouble with the law, is deeply rooted in
my desire to turn young people away from the life that
nearly captured me.

Like some of you, I know what it is like not to feel a father's
love. I know what it is like to be seething with anger, hurt
people and act out of pure emotion.

I always thought my father was disappointed with me
because I did not become a boxer like my older brother, or I
did not gamble like both brothers. I showed no enthusiasm
for five-card stud poker or betting on thoroughbred racing.
I thought he did not talk to me or spend time at home
because he simply did not love me.

It was a strange emotion I felt when Dad died. I was
twenty-two and instead of feeling grief, I felt relieved. I
thought, "At last the yelling and the arguments are over."
We would eventually have peace at home and the gambling
and betting at bookie joints had come to an end, I believed.

I was once trying to convince a ministry leader there was
corruption in his organization. I knew the FBI was
investigating him and members of his ministry. In
appealing to his need to clean up the bad behavior, I quoted
from a line from the movie *The Godfather*. Offering to put
aside files that would disclose internal corruption, I said, "I
want to make you an offer you can't refuse." The offer
meant repentance rather than disclosure.

It was serious and yet at the same time laughable that he
repeated the remark to friends saying, "He threatened my
life." When I heard how he had interpreted the quote, I said
to him, "Christ has changed my life. If I was a *'made man'*,
you would not be sitting here, you would have been
whacked." There was nervous laughter on his part but there
was complete truth in the statement. The way of the family
was retaliation. You go to the pay phone, call a guy named

Rocco, and he pays you a visit. The visit makes it clear what is expected of you, whether it is a payment or getting out of town. When the behavior continues, the guy comes back as part of a *welcome wagon*. Something gets broken, your kneecap, fingers or a leg. When the guy does not get the message, there is a contract put out and a stranger makes a *hit*. You end up six feet under.

Who was I going to become? The one carrying out the hit, or the one giving the order? In the family, you work your way up. When you hear the words *la Famiglia e'aperta* (the family is open), you are invited for life. From that point on, especially for a Sicilian, everything is done *in onere della Famiglia* (in honor of the family).

For many years, I never even hinted at the subjects in this book. It was something I tried to erase from my conscious memory and keep tightly locked in a small mental closet. After all, most people like to talk about relatives who have accomplished great things in life, those who have won awards, gifted artists, movie stars, writers, or a sportscaster, but not talk about brothers going to prison or making the headlines of a major newspaper for their crimes.

I did not want to discuss the Black Hand relatives who extorted each other, my great aunt charged with murder, or my great uncle Vito who was shot in the back of the head. Since we want people to think well of us, we keep the "black sheep" hidden away. Unfortunately, in my family, there was a herd of black sheep.

Very few people join the mob. You are born into it. Part of it is blood and ancestry, but you have to be vouched for, that is, recommended by someone already in the family. Then you are proposed. They check to make sure you are loyal and they test your loyalty by having you commit a hit. And when you are finally *made*, there is a ceremony. Sometimes they burn a holy card with the words *come si bruscia questa santa cosi'cis bucera la mia anima*, basically "as the saint burns, so will burn your soul." It is a warning. If you talk about family operations, you die.

It never occurred to me that it was out of the ordinary to be a bartender at eight years of age, walking in a haze of cigar smoke at midnight serving drinks to members of the mob.

I am not simply a historian. I am not a writer who went to the library and looked up the background of famous mobsters. They dined in my home. My mother danced with the "homicide squad." My grandfather worked for the Gennas producing illegal alcohol for Capone, and of the events they did not directly participate in, my family had direct knowledge. They heard conversations in the barbershop and conversations at the dinner table. They heard the real story of who committed the St. Valentine's Day massacre and the names of the drivers.

My father enjoyed going to the Villa Venice, but was it simply for the food or the fact that several blocks away Giancana had an illegal gambling casino where patrons were shuttled?

"The law is for dopes," my brother Joseph once said, "The key is not getting caught."

God delivered me from a world of secrets and violence, drinking, gambling, and crime as a way of life.

Clearly it was a great force that pulled me out of the family. As you have seen from the previous chapter, I have been greatly blessed. But following Christ does not come without a cost. When you take one road, you are rejecting another. Jesus himself made it very clear that you cannot live in two worlds at the same time. You cannot serve two masters. You will love one and hate the other. You cannot be a person who tells the truth and does good and simultaneously lie and do evil. One world will win. One lifestyle will choke out the other.

My family has not talked to me for over 20 years. I pray often for reconciliation, but I also understand the Sicilian vendetta and the stubbornness that my father had, which became a part of my brother's lives. They have hard hearts. It is unlikely they will change, but not impossible.

I know now that the closeness with my brothers that I so desired would have brought me into a life so different from the one I have lived. It would have been a life of deception and crime from which I never would have escaped.

There are things that we seek in life almost with desperation. We want them and we are frustrated when they are elusive, just out of reach. Sometimes we discover years later that some of the things we desired the most would have ruined our life. A philosopher from ancient Greece named Aristotle said that we should "seek the good life," that is a life of morality, clean ethics and spirituality. The opposite would be a bad life, one that is selfish, immoral and dishonest. God gave me the illumination many years ago to realize that the "bad life" would leave me empty and it would not be worth living. It is easier to follow the crowd. It is easier to have others make choices and decisions for us.

It takes no effort to seek what is comfortable. It takes no effort to capitulate to dark habits and wave a flag of surrender to evil.

Life is, after all, a fight, and the prize always goes to the honorable warrior. In the end, we have scars and wounds because we have fought against great odds, but the victory of eternal life does not go to those who sit on the sidelines, who merely observe, comment and criticize.

I have never regretted the decision to reject the money. While I am saddened by the consequences, I do not regret rejecting a family in crime. Giving my heart to God was the best thing I ever did! It has not always been an easy path, but it has been the right path.

I have peace in my soul that can only come from God. It is a wonderful thing not to wake up agitated, fearful, or depressed. God can do for you what he did for me. You have only to take that first step and trust His gift of eternal life purchased by the sacrifice of Jesus on a cross, through faith.

I still have problems in life, but I also have the resource of God's power bringing me joy each day.

Whether you, the reader, are young or old, let me say emphatically, it is never too late to live the life you should live. Remember, it takes courage to change.

It takes much courage to change greatly.